PARIS: A LOVE STORY

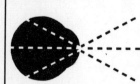

This Large Print Book carries the
Seal of Approval of N.A.V.H.

PARIS: A LOVE STORY

A MEMOIR

KATI MARTON

THORNDIKE PRESS
A part of Gale, Cengage Learning

DISCARD

GALE
CENGAGE Learning®

Detroit • New York • San Francisco • New Haven, Conn • Waterville, Maine • London

GALE
CENGAGE Learning®

LIBRARY OF CONGRESS CATALOGING-IN-PUBLICATION DATA

Marton, Kati.
 Paris : a love story : a memoir / by Kati Marton.
  pages ; cm. — (Thorndike Press large print biography)
  ISBN 978-1-4104-5358-7 (hardcover) — ISBN 1-4104-5358-8 (hardcover) 1. Marton, Kati. 2. Women authors, American—Biography. 3. Women journalists—United States—Biography. 4. Paris (France)—Biography. 5. Holbrooke, Richard C., 1941-2010. 6. Jennings, Peter, 1938-2005. 7. Large type books. I. Title.
PN4874.M198A3 2012b
070.92—dc23
[B]   2012032087

Published in 2012 by arrangement with Simon & Schuster, Inc.

Printed in the United States of America
1 2 3 4 5 6 7 16 15 14 13 12

Paris: A Love Story

Arc de Triomphe

Lancaster Hotel

rue de Berri

rue du Faubourg St-Honoré

Parc Monceau

Musée Camondo

Fouquet's

Élysée Palace

Champs-Élysées

Chez Francis

Grand Palais

Petit Palais

The Obelisk

The Tuileries

THE

Pont de la Concorde

SEINE

Pont Alexandre III

Eiffel Tower

blvd. St-Germain

rue de Grenelle

rue du Bac

MY PARIS

blvd. du

rue de

Mont

Parc des Buttes Chaumont

rue de Rivoli

place des Vosges

The Louvre

Bastille

place Dauphine

Café de Flore

Pont Neuf

place St-Germain

Notre-Dame

Église St-Germain-des-Prés

place St-Michel

blvd. St-Germain

Quai de la Tournelle

Pont Sully

rue de Bernardins

Odéon Theater

rue des Écoles

Vaugirard

Café le Rostand

The Sorbonne

My First Apartment

rue Monge

Luxembourg Gardens

blvd. St-Michel

My Present Apartment

The Paris Mosque

Parnasse

La Closerie des Lilas

For Richard
with love

■ ■ ■ ■

Part I

■ ■ ■ ■

If there is any substitute for love,
it is memory.
To memorize, then, is to restore intimacy.
— Joseph Brodsky

CHAPTER ONE

Like a human snowplow, I surge against the flow of chanting, banner-waving students pouring into the boulevard St.-Germain. I am determined to get to the Café de Flore before Richard does. My husband has flown all night from Kabul on a military plane. I am merely crossing from the fifth into the sixth arrondissement. As he shuttles between Washington, Kabul, and Islamabad, we have little time together; minutes matter. But this is the Latin Quarter, and it is October, the season of student *manifestations*. *Les manifs* are a routine feature of my Parisian neighborhood, and I usually enjoy their high-spirited revolutionary theater. Not today. The students have blocked traffic on St.-Germain and prevented Richard's car from reaching our apartment on the rue des Écoles.

Hot and sweaty, I arrive at the terrace of the Flore. Richard is already there and, as usual these days, he is on the phone. As he is looking up, his smile momentarily lifts travel fatigue from his features. "You're late!" he says, a hand covering the phone. He hangs up, and we kiss. Then we exhale in unison from sheer relief that we are together — and in Paris! That is how it has been for the past two years. Days stolen from a devouring job.

Richard takes out his frayed wallet to pay for our *citrons pressés*. "See," he says, "it's still here," a faded Polaroid of the two of us in the Tuileries Garden taken in 1994, wearing matching expressions of goofy happiness. "And I still have this," he says, proudly extracting the torn corner of a phone message pad with my sister's Paris telephone number. In 1993, he tracked me down with that number. His *amulette*. "You are a ridiculously sentimental man," I tell him.

Holding hands, we navigate between the green street cleaning machines that are already vacuuming up the debris of the street protest, as we make our way to the rue des Écoles. We have one night together. He will fly to Brussels the next day for a conference he has called on Afghanistan and Pakistan.

On this balmy fall afternoon, we are not thinking about that. It always feels right to meet in the city where we began our life together. Paris is also roughly midway between Washington and the world's bleakest conflict zone, Richard's diplomatic beat. Climbing the narrow, creaky stairs to our pied-à-terre reminds us of other lives we have lived — and lives we planned still to live. In Paris, we wrap our little apartment around ourselves like a blanket, and keep the world outside, barely leaving our village tucked in the shadow of the Pantheon. Tonight we have to.

I am in Paris not only to see my husband but also to launch the French edition of my new book. My book party at the American Embassy is the next night, and it will be the first such event that Richard will not attend. On this, our only evening together, we are dining with Ambassador Charles Rivkin and his wife, Susan Tolson, the hosts of my book event.

Entering the Left Bank restaurant a few hours later, we smile at the sight of a giant poster of my book cover on the glass front door. Several diners acknowledge Richard's presence with discreet nods. He and I exchange looks of mutual pleasure and pride.

I recall a lurking feeling that things were going too well for us last year. My new book had the best reviews I ever had and I had been named a National Book Critics Circle finalist. Our children were leading productive lives, Lizzie working for the United Nations in Haiti, Chris writing his first book, Richard's sons, David and Anthony, grown, with beautiful children of their own. Richard had the toughest assignment of his career, but it was work he loved.

I am not a prayerful person. But I recall praying in mid-2010, Please God, don't let anything bad happen to us. This is my superstitious Hungarian side, that you are punished if you are too happy. When my late-night fears circled, my first thought was for my children. My husband was indestructible. He would always be there to pick up the pieces.

The distant war reaches out for Richard even during dinner. His phone rings and he leaves the table to talk. His soufflé — the restaurant's specialty — is cold and flat when he returns. His phone rings again and he answers again. This time I scold him. "You are being rude." He glowers at me and squeezes my hand hard. "You have no idea what's going on," he answers. "There is always something going on," I protest. The ambassador notes Richard's grip and shoots his wife a look. My husband catches himself.

"Try this." He offers me a forkful of his freshly remade cheese soufflé. A peace offering. I shake my head. "Oh please, it's so good," he coaxes me. I relent and he does not answer the next call.

Walking home from the rue de Sèvres, we stop in front of the beautiful Romanesque church of St.-Germain-des-Prés, which anchors this neighborhood. But his phone rings again and I am left to remember alone when I first learned about Romanesque churches from Richard, seventeen years ago, when we fell in love in this city.

I get up early the next morning. He appears a few hours later, looking sheepish and like an unkempt boy. "You are so disciplined," he says, finding me with my nose in a book, taking notes. "I have to be," I answer. "I am not as quick as you. Come," I say, patting the couch where I am sprawled. "Let's read together." Richard has two books in his briefcase, which have traveled back and forth to Afghanistan with him for months: Rudyard Kipling's *Kim* and John le Carré's *Our Kind of Traitor*. "No, I'm going to buy you a new outfit for your book party," he announces.

Both books are still on his nightstand in the rue des Écoles — unfinished.

Shopping in Paris is one of our rituals. It is the only place in the world Richard enjoys shopping. Our closets are full of Parisian purchases spanning the last decade and a half. In a chic Right Bank boutique, I parade several beautiful suits and dresses. Richard looks up from the phone and nods at the velvet suit I am modeling. "That color looks good on you," he says. "C'est aubergine, monsieur," the saleslady interjects. Richard has spotted some shoes of the same shade and, still on the phone, signals the lady to bring those, too. I decline the cashmere overcoat, the color of cream, that he drapes on my shoulder. "Let's get a coffee," I say, our time together nearly up.

On the rue de Rivoli, we squeeze into a crowded café terrace, Richard looking for shade, me for a sunny spot. "I'm sorry I can't stay for your book party," he says. "That's the end of your perfect attendance record for four books," I answer. "But you know I came just to be with you," he says. "It won't always be like this," he promises. The black embassy car is at the curb; the driver is holding the door open. We kiss. It is our last time together in Paris.

From the café on the rue de Rivoli it is a short stroll to the W. H. Smith bookstore, where I now head. On the front table I see

Bob Woodward's new book, *Obama's Wars*. I buy a copy and head back out into the October sunshine. At the Tuileries Garden, across the street, I pull up a wrought-iron chair and flip to the index. Holbrooke, R.: a great many listings. I turn to the one that also lists me. A wave of anger and disbelief washes over me as I read. According to Woodward, the president soured on Richard when my husband asked him to call him Richard, not Dick, at the ceremony appointing him special representative for Afghanistan and Pakistan. "For Kati," Richard explained, "who is in the audience, and who doesn't like 'Dick.' "

How could the president — who once requested that his friends not call him "Barry" — hold this against Richard? I am too agitated to sit for another minute in the sunny gardens. Embarrassed that I made such a big deal of my preference for Richard over Dick, a fact I made clear to him the minute we met, in 1985. Angry that such a trivial matter would turn the president against the man he just assigned his toughest foreign policy job. And then, as I head toward the Seine and home, I am overwhelmed by love for a man who would use his precious one-on-one with the commander in chief to ask a favor, for his wife!

No wonder he never mentioned the Wood-ward book, nor brought a copy home. He was trying to protect me — as always. I have an urge to run after the limousine speeding him now to a military base outside Paris — to tell him I love him, one more time.

Aside from my superstitious fear that things were going too well for us, there were no signs, no portents of tragedy looming. He played tennis over Thanksgiving weekend in Southampton. We did a marathon of mov-ies, his favorite pastime. But if I believed in signs, there was one. As Richard packed to return to Washington on that Sunday, he searched frantically for his wallet. We looked in all the usual places, emptied all pockets in his closet, and moved the bed and chest of drawers. No sign. Oh well, he said, it'll turn up. It always has.

I returned to New York, Richard to Wash-ington. Every time he called, he asked if his wallet had turned up. There was no money in it. He had already canceled his credit cards and replaced his security passes. Still, he was agitated that it had not turned up, as it always had in the past. Why are you so upset? I finally asked him. "It's the picture of us in the Tuileries, and your sister's telephone number," he said. "I've had them since 1994." The wallet has still not turned up. Like Richard, it disappeared.

He disappeared. That is how it seems to me. I had assumed that death would be a gradual transition, a passage after long illness, and sad, unhurried good-byes. Not a midlife thunderclap.

One and a half hours before his collapse we were making our Christmas plans on the phone. We were finally getting away. I made him laugh when I described an incident in the news about an overzealous Homeland Security agent at LaGuardia, accused of groping by a diplomat we did not particularly like. An international incident was in the making — though compared to the life-and-death issues on which Richard spent every waking hour, a minor one. "Oh, it feels so good to laugh," Richard said. Just one more week, I said. "Well, don't bother coming to Washington this weekend," he said. "I'll be at the White House for the president's year-end review. Got to go meet with David Axelrod at the White House, then Hillary at State. Love you."

Love you, too.

When he called an hour and a half later I barely recognized his voice. "I feel a pain I have never felt," he said from the ambulance, en route to the George Washington

University Hospital emergency room. This voice of deep pain was not one I had ever heard. "I have no feeling in my legs," he said. There was fear in my husband's voice. "I am on my way!" I shouted over the siren's wail. Those were my last words to Richard.

CHAPTER TWO

The days and weeks that followed seem long ago. Grief distorts everything — time included. Even as I reeled from shock, the explosion of love and the tributes from all corners of the globe were a balm. Richard was a big man — in every sense of the word. Controversy was bound to dog such a large personality. Throughout his career he collided with more cautious public servants. But all of that seemed washed away now by a general disbelief at the death of such a vividly *alive* man.

As the wife of such a public man, my grief could not stay private. My husband was still fighting for his life following twenty-one hours of surgery to repair a dissected aorta when our friend Samantha Power, my constant companion during those days, persuaded me to leave the hospital to attend Mass with her and her three-year-old son. (I remember her babysitter gave me a

St. Christopher medal, which is still in my coat pocket.) Almost the minute we sat down in the pew, my phone rang. I slipped outside to Pennsylvania Avenue to take a call from the president of Afghanistan, Hamid Karzai. "Mrs. Holbrooke," he said, "we are praying for your husband's speedy recovery." I thanked him politely. After seventeen years with Richard, I knew not to waste a second with this key figure in the conflict for which my husband had given of his last measure. "You know, Mr. President, this is more than a job for Richard. It is his mission. He genuinely loves your country and your people too," I said to the man with whom Richard had a famously fractious relationship. "Well, we need him back here, Mrs. Holbrooke," Karzai said. "He must get better." I thought I detected something akin to genuine emotion in his voice — but maybe I just wanted to.

As I headed back to the church, my phone rang again. The State Department Operations Center announced that Pakistan's president, Asif Zardari, was on the line. "Kati!" he greeted me, for we had met. "I told Richard he was overdoing it! He must take it easy. He was traveling too much, and to such terrible places. Oh, I am so sorry. But he will be better. He is a strong man and we are all praying for him." Zardari sounded like an old friend. Genuinely concerned. Human to human.

The third call as Samantha, her son Declan, and I were leaving the church was from President Obama. "Michelle and I are praying for you both," the president said. "Richard is a strong man. He'll pull through. We need him back." The next time I left the tightly sealed world of the hospital was to attend a State Department event at which both President Obama and the secretary of state were to speak about Richard. It was a holiday party for the diplomatic corps, and Christmas carolers were circling around dignitaries and their spouses in their festive attire. I had changed my clothes for the first time since Richard was admitted, but I neither looked nor felt festive. There was still hope then, but not enough to make the sound of "Jingle Bells" anything but jarring. I felt utterly disembodied as I shook hands with State Department colleagues of Richard's and led our children into the ornate reception room of the secretary of state. Hillary was her warm, compassionate self. She had spent hours at the hospital, often silently holding my hand as we sat waiting. It was no effort to be with someone who loved Richard as much as she did. President Obama spoke eloquently to the gathered diplomats, calling Richard the greatest diplomat of his generation, now fighting for his life. Then the president took time to speak with me and each of our four children. I have White House photographs recording this event, but subsequent events have erased the memory of what he said to me.

As we set off from the State Department for the short walk back to the hospital, a black official SUV pulled up. "Mrs. Holbrooke," the driver said, "I am with the FBI and I was attached to your husband's security detail in Kabul. Let me drive you back to GW." We all climbed in, and now I wish I had noted the agent's name. He was there when everything turned and he was a kind man.

My cell rang. "Hello, Kati, this is Farzad Najam." "Oh hello," I answered, trying to sound bright. "Which paper are you with," I asked, having been told Pakistani journalists were waiting at the hospital to interview me about Richard's condition. "Kati, this is Dr. Najam," he said. "Oh, I apologize, Doctor," I said, my tone slipping. Lulled by the surreal holiday party and the presidential attention, for just a moment I had stopped thinking about the doctors and the vigil in the ICU. "How far are you?" Dr. Najam asked. "A few minutes away," I answered. "Okay, then. See you when you get back," he said. I suppose my body language gave me away, for, though I said nothing, the previously talkative agent fell silent and picked up speed.

We trooped into the windowless room set aside for the family on the ICU floor. Dr. Najam and his team were waiting there. "Mrs. Holbrooke." The handsome Pakistani cardiologist was now formal and, for the first time, unsmiling. "Richard is telling us he wants to go."

I dropped my head in my hands for a minute or two. The room was very quiet. Then I followed the doctor to the ICU. "Take your time," he said. "Take all the time you like." The ICU felt different now. The feverish activity of the past three days had ceased. With the machines turned off, it was as quiet as a battlefield after defeat. The doctors and nurses looked grim and deflated, as they silently removed their masks. I said a few loving words to Richard, but he was no longer my Richard. Life leaves the body so quickly.

Our children followed. David, Anthony, Elizabeth, and Chris each said his own good-bye.

I crossed the hospital's lobby, where hundreds of people had gathered — a blur of outstretched arms and tear-stained faces. How had word spread so fast?

Admiral Michael Mullen in his impressive uniform, and his wife, Debbie, gave us a lift to our Georgetown house. The chairman of the Joint Chiefs carried Richard's clothes in what looked like a garbage bag. Samantha and her husband, Cass Sunstein, arrived with Thai food. We wept and drank and laughed for the rest of the long night, and told the stories we will be telling forever. None of us believed he was gone — least of all me. I don't remember feeling anything at all.

CHAPTER THREE

I awoke from a drugged few hours of sleep the next morning with the same question I would ask every morning for the next few months. Did I dream this? But the worse I feel, the more decisive I tend to be. So I announced to my children and siblings, We're packing up the house. I don't want to come back to this place. So, still in our pajamas, using the bubble wrap and boxes provided by Richard's assistants, we set to work.

An hour or so into our packing, President Bill Clinton dropped by, unannounced. Settling into an easy chair and, with his legendary gift for consoling the stricken on full display, he spun tales of the man he called "Holbrooke." I loved the one of Richard coming to "interview" him in Little Rock to see if he was fit to run for president. Or the one of "Holbrooke" telling him exactly where to sit at various Balkan conferences for maximum impact. "Seating or negotiating — he always had a plan," the president said. "Smartest man I ever met," he said, as his eyes filled with unshed tears. And then, just as suddenly as he arrived, Clinton glanced at his watch and said, "Look at the time!" and then announced, "I have to go to Haiti," and off he went.

We resumed packing. By day's end, I pulled the door of the N Street house shut behind me for the last time. It had been our sanctuary and we had been happy there. I forced myself to turn around. The familiar lemon-yellow door pulled me back up the front stairs. I looked up and down the tranquil Georgetown street, as I did each morning when I stepped out to get the newspapers. I want to feel this now, I told myself. I want to remember. It was dark and cold when we headed for Union Station and back to New York.

CHAPTER FOUR

My family got me through Christmas. My sister and brother, my two children and nephews never left me for a single day or night. My sister cooked Hungarian dishes she learned from our mother and grandmother, while my brother played the piano. My children, grieving still for their father who died four years before, understood what I was going through: shock, alternating with high spirits at having the people I most loved near me. Sleepless nights left me groggy and weepy all day. Somehow, the snow that kept falling, wrapping the world in shades of gray and muffling the noisy city, helped. So did my nephew Mathieu's newborn, Lucien. We bought a sleigh and took turns pulling him in Central Park. Hours spent digging our car out from under fresh mountains of snow were a welcome distraction. Mostly we did what families whose lives have suddenly been upended do: we talked about past Christmases, with Richard, with Mama and Papa, and with my children's father, Peter. The Missing.

After the Christmas holidays, I returned to Washington for Richard's memorial at the Kennedy Center. One week before his death, he and I had crossed the same red-carpeted lobby to attend Washington's most glamorous annual event, the Kennedy Center Honors. The capital's entire establishment turns out for this, Washington's equivalent of the Oscars. Holding hands, we greeted senators and cabinet members. Suddenly Richard noticed the bulky silhouette of a man standing alone, the space around him cleared. The capital's way of marking a *nonperson*. C'mon, Richard said, pulling me toward Congressman Charles Rangel. "Hey, Charlie," Richard said to the freshly disgraced congressman facing ethics charges. "Let me introduce my wife, Kati." After some idle chatter, we took our leave of Rangel. Richard, a veteran of Washington's sometimes cruel local customs, often said it's the people who are suddenly down and out that we always have to be nice to. It's easy to be nice to those on the up-and-up.

Greeting scores of friends and colleagues, we made our way to our seats. I am trying now to recall how good it felt to be part of our couple. Just a few months before, we had been honored by the Asia Society as one of five Great Couples. How long ago it now seems. In accepting the award, I had said I had no idea how I would get anything done without Richard's support.

One month after that glittering evening, as I held tight to my children's hands, we entered the Kennedy Center. I noticed a tall, blond woman, alone and hunched inside her black coat. In Washington you notice people who are trying *not* to be noticed at public events. Diane Sawyer — Richard's partner for many years before I came into his life. She had written me the briefest and most generous note. "At the core of Richard Holbrooke," Diane wrote, "was his deep love for you." I walked over to her to say thank you. Tears were streaming down her face and we exchanged a wordless embrace.
  Our friend George Stevens, the producer of the Kennedy Center Honors, organized the memorial and it was remarkable. What President Obama, President Clinton and Secretary of State Clinton, Admiral Mullen, and former UN secretary-general Kofi Annan said about Richard belongs in the history books. Renée Fleming sang "Ave

Maria" at my request and I have rarely heard anything so piercingly, heartbreakingly beautiful. Backstage, as we waited to speak, I stood with President Obama, his arm around my shoulder, looking at a photomontage of Richard projected on the stage. What struck me was how much older Richard looked in the final months than even a year before. Pictures of him with Karzai in Kabul, with various generals in Islamabad, in refugee camps and on military bases, showed a man aging before our eyes. When he was home he was happy and relaxed and I was too busy enjoying our brief reunions to notice. "He aged so much on this job," I exclaimed. Later, I hoped the president did not take that as a rebuke. He told me he had worked on his eulogy late into the night, looking for the perfect poem by Yeats — Richard's favorite. He was warm and easy to be with. "Well," he said looking out at the packed Kennedy Center, "this tribute may even exceed Richard's expectations."

I spoke at this and the other two memorials. His death had made me feel helpless. However painful, speaking about Richard was something within my power, something I could *do*.

I had another reason for speaking. Most

people knew Richard for his intelligence, his appetite for work and for friendship. He shared very little of his personal life — even when he was with his close friends. I wanted to fill in that missing dimension. "Richard was a very good husband," I said at the Kennedy Center. "There were no boundaries between our personal and professional lives. We gave each other great courage — knowing the other was always there. Not a single day passed — wherever he was — without a phone call."

Nor did we ever go to sleep on a quarrel, I thought, but I did not say this.

After the memorial, at the reception on the roof of the Kennedy Center, I shook thousands of hands. Foreign ministers, generals, ambassadors, and old friends who had traveled far to be there; I didn't reach them all.

But my day was not yet over. The American ambassador to Afghanistan, General Karl Eikenberry, called on me at my hotel. "Our embassy — the largest in the world — is Richard's creation," he said, presenting me with the Stars and Stripes, which had flown half-mast over the Kabul embassy. "General Petraeus will present you the flag which flew half-mast over NATO headquarters." I thanked him for making the long trip from Kabul to Washington to honor Richard. Some time later, the Speaker of the House, Nancy Pelosi, presented me with the flag that had flown half-mast over the Capitol the day he died. I was moved beyond words by these gestures for a deeply patriotic man.

Pakistan's president Zardari, who had traveled from Islamabad to attend the memorial, arrived next. I was spent from hours of publicly shared grief, but rather than an empty audience between a head of state and a new widow, this turned into a heartfelt conversation between a widow and a widower. Zardari, his eyes filled with emotion, talked about his own grief after his wife Benazir Bhutto's assassination. "You must let yourself feel the pain, Kati," he advised me, like an old friend. "It is good. I have not touched anything in Benazir's room," he said. "Her saris still hang in her closet. Her beads are where she left them on her dresser."

We were joined by Pakistan's ambassador to Washington, Husain Haqqani. His wife lives in Islamabad, and he was clearly affected by this unusually personal exchange. He said, "Mr. President, I would like to spend more time with my wife in the future." Zardari smiled and said, "Yes, Husain, you should do that." Then, in the only political note of this surprisingly personal exchange, Zardari said, "What a bad bargain Pakistan made — nurturing extremists to fight India and the Soviets." He shook his head. "Now we are stuck with them."

I have never used Richard's last name, but after the Washington memorial, I reserved a table for my family at our favorite restaurant under "Richard Holbrooke." I now understood widows who change their names to their husband's; anything to draw the memory closer.

CHAPTER FIVE

After the memorials in Washington and at the United Nations in New York, I tried to pick up the thread of my life. The life that we had built was over. I felt cut loose from my moorings — unprotected. Who was I, if not part of a couple? My kids were grown up; Lizzie was in Haiti with only an intermittent phone connection. ("Are you ok Mom?" was a regular text message from my daughter, which made me smile.) Chris was in Brooklyn, loving and concerned. But I do not want to lean on them. I want my own life back.

For months letters arrive each day — in the end there are thousands of them. Most describe specific memories of interaction with Richard. Planted on our living room floor, I keep reading, as they deserve to be read, carefully, and frequently with tears. Some have a tiny crown on the back of the envelope, denoting a royal sender. Others are written on paper torn from a notebook. I feel as if the sender is writing for his or her own sake, as well as mine. To capture something — a moment, a conversation, an impression, the advice Richard dispensed so freely — that will not come again.

A handwritten note addressed to Mrs. Richard C. Holbrooke in the tiniest handwriting I have ever seen is dropped off at my apartment. "I woke up this morning," the note says, "and thought of you, and of all the mornings you will wake up without Richard. Signed, Joan Didion." I am moved by this touching but infinitely sad note. But I don't want to be sad on all the mornings to come. I have just been made painfully aware of how fleeting life is and how unpredictable. In a sense, I have never wanted to hold life tighter, or to live more fully than now, reeling from loss.

I see photos of myself *before*, and I look different: innocent and trusting. The look of someone who just assumed nothing bad would ever happen to her. I know I have to get through these days — each of which brings a tidal wave of grief at unexpected moments. On Fridays I still expect him to blast through the front door and call out, "Katika!" using my Hungarian diminutive. He was not a quiet man. And now the apartment is so quiet.

So. My life must be reinvented. No living backward. No living forward. Living in the present. But first: faced squarely. He really isn't coming back. There will never be anyone else like him. No one will ever challenge, amuse, provoke, or (occasionally) annoy me, nor so *get* me ever again. The days and weeks seem only to clarify my loss. Who to share with the minute triumphs and tiny slights — imagined or real? When I write something, I want to show him. Who else cares as much as he did?

I pretend that I can make a new life happen, by sheer willpower. I fly to Seattle to address several hundred people in the town hall of Yakima. Other than the memorials, this is my first public appearance since Richard's death. I ask the lady who is to introduce me to mention that fact, in case I stumble. I am mortified to hear her announce, "Kati would like you to know this is the first time she is speaking in public since the death of her husband and that we are grateful that she made the trip." And of course midway through my speech Richard's shadow passes and my voice breaks. A hush falls over the hall as the good people of Yakima hold their collective breath and wait for me to compose myself. The speech is a success. I even tour vineyards and orchards. (What are the chances I will ever be back here? A question I now frequently ask myself.)

I have made it through the speech, the book signing, and the shaking of hundreds of hands. But at the Seattle airport, I learn my flight home is delayed by several hours and no longer direct. Hot waves of anxiety wash over me. I do not want to cry. No one to call to vent to. No one who will tell me this is no big deal. Go get a beer and chill out. I close my eyes and breathe deeply, as if I were back in the delivery room, giving birth. I do not want to be led away by Homeland Security. I am not yet myself.

The weeks pass and still every damn thing is a memory. My daughter and I watch *Z*, the great Costa-Gavras thriller. I had never before thought to compare the Yves Montand character, the crusading politician who is assassinated, to Richard. But now it's obvious. How different the charismatic public man is from the very human private one. How painfully familiar it feels, watching Montand's newly widowed wife, surrounded by cameras and journalists and fighting for composure, or her blank look when her husband's followers assure her his work will survive him. What are you talking about, her look seems to say. He is gone.

Watching an old favorite, *Shoot the Piano Player*, I am transfixed by Charlie, brilliantly played by Charles Aznavour. He has absorbed multiple losses, and at the end is still playing the piano. That's me! I am Charlie the piano player.

Another trip. Another speech. This one is in Berlin, where I am to address a conference of Human Rights Watch. At JFK Airport's Lufthansa counter, I am handed a card to fill out for notification of next of kin. I don't fill it out. My welfare is no longer an urgent matter to anyone. Bad news will reach them soon enough.

Berlin is Richard's city. He was ambassador here when we first fell in love. Getting off the plane's gangway at Tegel Airport, I remember when he stood there waiting for me, like a kid on Christmas morning. Facing an audience of human rights activists, students, and the American ambassador, I speak about Richard's brand of diplomacy. One human at a time.

I am Charlie, the piano player.

Some time later, I face a tougher audience in Washington, the city I most fear for all the memories of the last two years, and of Richard's last days. But it is the city I most want to remind of Richard's legacy. I address the annual dinner of Refugees International, an NGO he once chaired. As I enter the hall, I know I have been here before. When? Then I remember: A dance. Katharine Graham's seventieth birthday party. I have no memory of what it was like to flirt, to dance, to feel anything at all beyond sadness.

Surrounded by Richard's admirers, mostly young people whose stories all seem to begin with "Because of Richard, I decided to . . . ," I begin to relax. I introduce two old friends of Richard's to each other: Farooq Kathwari, the Kashmiri-American CEO of Ethan Allen Furniture, and the literary critic and editor Leon Wieseltier. "My father was a salesman for Ethan Allen," Leon tells Farooq. America! What a great country. Richard would love this. I am enjoying myself. These are "his" people.

From the stage, I thank the outpouring of affection, "*Love*, actually," I correct myself, and stumble over the word. Silence falls in the auditorium. Love is what I feel for the absent man. It does not seem possible that here, in *his* town in the company of *his* people, *he* is gone. I am followed to the podium by Vermont senator Patrick Leahy, who receives a lifetime award for his support for refugees. The senator tells an amusing story of a trip to Kosovo with Richard. Everybody laughs and Richard is suddenly very much present. Afterward, Leahy tells me, "You know, Hillary called me at my farm in Vermont, to tell me he had died. She was crying on the phone," he says.

I am suddenly filled with such warmth for the secretary of state, who never lost her composure in the hospital when she sat there silently, keeping me company. She remained steady and controlled when she eulogized Richard at the Kennedy Center, and a few weeks later at the American Academy in Berlin. Somehow, I am relieved to hear that to her old friend Pat Leahy she allowed the tears to flow.

Back in New York, I look out at snowy Central Park through a curtain of ice and rain — a perfect filter between the world and me. It is a winter of record snowfall, which suits me fine.

In February, a daylong seminar on the Dayton Accords, which ended the war in Bosnia in 1995 and was Richard's proudest diplomatic achievement, is held at New York University. I introduce myself for the first time as Richard Holbrooke's widow. Another watershed.

Presidents' Day weekend. I wake up with

44

a new feeling. What lives I have lived in the past seventeen years! How enriched I am in every way. I am starting to use the first person singular for the first time in my adult life. I am going to be all right. I feel a surge of energy. I decide to attack Richard's closet — still crammed full of his things. At the sight of the blue cashmere blazer we bought on our final Parisian shopping trip, I break down. No, I am not ready to go through his closet yet. Grief is not a linear process. It hits you with a force when you least expect it.

I recall my mother, in her communist prison, facing a long sentence, and cut off from her husband and her young children. In her lowest moments, she forced herself to do sit-ups in her tiny cell. So now, with my friends mostly out of town for the long weekend, with another ice storm pummeling the city, I put my bathing suit on under my snow pants and parka and head to my health club's swimming pool. This is what Mama would do, I tell myself. I recall my father's letter from the same prison. "Once before," Papa wrote, recalling what the Nazis had done to our family, "we lost everything." My parents survived — and rebuilt their lives. So will I.

Late one night a few days later, my cell phone rings. This is the precise time when Richard would call from wherever he was, to say good night. "The State Department Operations Center calling," the voice informs me, as his calls did. For an instant, my heart skips a beat. "Secretary Clinton would like to speak with you," the operator announces.

Hillary is calling to let me know she is about to announce Richard's successor. Our friend Marc Grossman, an able diplomat, a good choice. "I wanted you to hear it from me, and not from the papers," she says. "Marc has no illusions about replacing Richard." Then, she adds, "You know, the White House now realizes what Richard was trying to do."

I thank her for another act of kindness, in a long string of them.

He was away so much, my friends say. You must be used to being alone. But I never felt alone. Our conversation, begun in Paris seventeen years ago, ended abruptly on December 13. *I am loved, therefore I am.* That was me. Now who am I? Why did no one tell me that we have love on loan? People should be told this. It is not the grand romantic moments that forge a

46

couple. Those are easy, and they pass. It is the daily, granular sharing of the most trivial details of life — of little or no interest to anyone else — that forged our bond. The freedom to share my least worthy thought, knowing that even when we disagreed, he was on my side.

In March, a postcard addressed to Ambassador Richard C. Holbrooke from the Democratic National Committee arrives in the mail. "Your membership has expired," the message reads. "We need you back."

I am having lunch at a café near Columbia University with an old friend. She is full of plans and ideas, fellowships and teaching jobs for me. I am getting excited about life. A lady at the next table leans over. "Excuse me for interrupting," she says, "but that was the most beautiful memorial I have ever seen." I am taken aback so she says, "I saw it on C-SPAN and recognized you. Your husband was a great man." Thank you, I say and get up to go to the ladies' room. "Somewhere Over the Rainbow" is playing on the bathroom speaker. A nice jazzy version. I had never realized it is a sad song. It's really about death. "Somewhere" is really about Nowhere. And only in death do "troubles melt like lemon drops." I start crying — not weeping, but crying really hard. I cannot go back out there. I lock the door and let the sobs pour out in waves. The weeks of public composure at wakes, memorials, and speeches — washed away by an old song.

I need to get away. Paris seems the right place. It is where Richard and I started our lives together and lived our happiest times. But, well before that, it is where I became who I am. In a life of multiple uprootings, Paris has been my one fixed point. Once before, I found happiness and beauty in Paris. I was a young girl then, the child of political refugees who settled in America. I longed for the interrupted European childhood. Someone once said that we breathe in our first language. Though my English vocabulary is far richer now, I learned French and Hungarian simultaneously as a child in Budapest. In Paris I found proximity to all that we were forced to abandon.

Of course I am no longer young. Richard's death has made me more sharply conscious of time's passing. Paris is the place where good things seem to happen to me.

In a way, every story with Paris at its heart is a love story. So is mine. It is where I fell in love, first with the city, then with the man who became the father of my children.

Then, in middle age, I found lasting love in Paris with Richard.

So, in Paris, I will relearn how to live.

■ ■ ■ ■

PART II

■ ■ ■ ■

That was the end of the first part of Paris. Paris was never to be the same again although it was always Paris and you changed and it changed.
— Ernest Hemingway, *A Moveable Feast*

CHAPTER SIX

Along with bottomless grief, death brings a rich bounty of practical problems. I decide to sell my home of twenty-five years. The Central Park West apartment, which once housed four people, is much too big for me, and too crowded with the ghosts of past lives. Nor can I afford it. I do not let myself imagine what it will actually feel like to pack up twenty-five years of accumulated life and pull another door shut behind me. During this first year after Richard's death, I am not looking for more pain. But I have to start pruning. This is akin to an archeological expedition. The visible part of our home, consisting of furniture, pictures, and books, is just the most recent layer of civilization. There are invisible layers beneath. I begin in our building's storage room. There, under the broken cane chair from our Budapest apartment, wedged between my ex-husband Peter Jennings's grandfather's sea chest and

53

Richard's ancient ski boots, is a plastic storage bin. The label, in my father's handwriting, says "Kati — Paris Letters."

So my parents saved those long-ago missives! Of course they would. We left so much behind when we abandoned our homeland in 1957. They weren't about to toss out any precious mementos of our new lives in America. My father spent his final year living here with Richard and me after my mother's death. This box must have accompanied him from Washington. In those days (only five years ago!) I was living my life on fast-forward and paid little attention to dusty boxes of youthful correspondence I did not plan on ever opening. Now I do. Along with my letters to my parents, there is a cardboard file shoved in the bin. "Kati's Letters to Peter," the large manila envelope says. While the letters to my parents are typed on onionskin using the Olivetti typewriter that was Papa's parting gift to me when I left for Paris, my letters to Peter are handwritten on blue airline stationery, on flights mostly to and from Paris. Hence their place in the Paris bin. Peter returned these letters to me when we parted after fifteen years of marriage.

Hands and jeans covered in dust, I pick up the box and let the iron bars of the storage room clang shut behind me.

Upstairs, I start reading.

I am meeting a young girl — neither child nor yet woman — plunging into life on her own. A time and a place I had long forgotten, rush in with her. At eighteen, I was avid for life and unprepared for the dramas to come.

"I just spotted the coast of Normandy!" I wrote my parents on September 11, 1967. I was traveling with a group of American students aboard the *Queen Mary*. "I know I feel differently from everyone around me, I can tell by their lack of fire," I wrote at the sight of my old continent for the first time in a decade.

I suppose what separated me from the thousands of other American students who come to Paris to finish their education or "find themselves" is that Paris felt like a homecoming to me. It was just a couple of hours' flight, a day by rail, from Budapest. But in those Cold War days, I could not even dream of returning to Budapest, the place of my interrupted childhood.

On February 25, 1955, at two in the morning, following a game of bridge at the home of the United States military attaché, six agents of the Hungarian secret police abducted my father from a street corner near our Budapest home. My mother and sister and I did not know where he had been taken, but in those days when terror ruled Soviet-occupied Hungary, arrests were common. My parents' professions as the last independent journalists in the country made them obvious targets of the state. I recall the night of my father's arrest as the end of my childhood. I have never let go of the image of secret police agents ripping up our apartment in search of evidence against my parents, while my sister and I hid in our parents' bed.

Four months later, our doorbell rang, and I answered it. Several men in workers' overalls peered down at me. "We came about the meter," one of them lied. "Your mother has rung. Please get her." I had a feeling they weren't who they said they were. Even to my six-year-old's eyes these men did not belong in those too clean overalls. But I was eager to return to my playmate in the next room. "Mama!" I called out, and returned to my friend. Even now, decades later, I feel guilty about my mother's arrest. I had called out to her too casually when her jailers came for her.

I did not see my mother for almost a year and my father for almost two years. They were held in the same maximum-security prison, convicted of spying for the United States. My sister and I were placed in the care of strangers, paid to look after us. Even after we were reunited as a family and began our long journey to freedom in America, nothing was ever the same again. That brutal separation from my parents at such an early age left a deep mark.

A decade of life of relative ease as a Hungarian refugee in suburban Washington, D.C., had not erased those memories.

"I'm home!" I wrote my parents at the sight of the European coastline. "10 years wiped away!"

My introduction to French life was in the ancient city of Tours, in the Loire valley. It helped that I already spoke the language. French had been drilled into me during my Hungarian childhood by a starchy French woman we called "Madame." She and I did not like each other. I could not persuade my parents that she was too impatient to be our nanny. My mother was determined that we should learn French, even in communist Hungary, where Russian was the mandatory second language. Now, having read the secret police files on my parents, I am vindicated in my early judgment of Madame. She was an agent of the AVO, the Hungarian KGB, using my sister and me as her informants. She did, however, teach me French, and did plant the seed, which in Tours first began to flower.

Annoyingly mixing French, English, and Hungarian in the first of my weekly letters home, I described my impressions: "The narrow winding streets, the aroma of fresh bread, the sound of pure French and the Cathedral down the street from where I live on the rue Jules Simon, flowers *partout*." A late adolescent inhaling beauty, I was electric with excitement at being in Europe again. "The whole way of life is so different from what we have become used to in the US," I wrote my mother and father. "It just feels much more natural for me. People live and talk and *enjoy* everything: flowers, food, wine — without shame. How different from the puritanical lives of so many Americans of comparable means! — just so they can save up for a new car or TV. Here, crumbling shacks are covered with flower boxes and rich and poor carry their fresh *baguette* and wine home from work."

Lodged in a so-called *maison particulière*, a historic townhouse belonging to the faded aristocratic descendants of the Renaissance painter François Clouet, I preened at how smoothly I fit in with such august company. "The Clouets are wonderful people and I have met few families with whom I can be so totally and uninhibitedly myself. I can be almost as '*szemtelen*' [Hungarian for fresh] with Baron Clouet as I am with you, Papa, and he even seems to enjoy it. They tell me that they've never met anyone like me, especially an American! — without any shyness and with opinions on every subject," I boasted. "Somehow, I feel a closeness — meeting of minds and spirits — with the Clouets and with other French people I have met — that I seldom feel with Americans."

There was nothing that did not enchant me about French life. "The Clouets have not changed their life style since before the Revolution," I wrote my parents on October 8. "Every weekend, Monsieur le Baron and his three sons perform the ritual of *La Chasse*, hunting. Then we have *gibier* [pheasant, rabbit, all kinds of strange birds] deliciously prepared, for the rest of the week. Madame la Baroness does even less than her husband," I wrote, seemingly full of admiration. "It's absolutely incredible to an American [which I have become] that these people can spend so much time, talking, eating, knitting, and giving orders to servants — now there is an art!" I marveled.

"The week's most pleasant afternoon I spent at the château of an impoverished Count and Countess. They make their living entirely off the land and don't have a car. Or a radio! But their *salon* is filled with masterpieces, and their land stretches for miles on a promontory overlooking the Loire. We sat on the grass surrounded by their *moutons* and horses, eating fruit from their trees and watching the sun set on the Loire. Really, it's the simplest things in life that are most pleasurable to me — eating an apple in the sunset with sheep and a crumbling old Count and his château. Sometimes just walking home from classes when it's getting dark, and inhaling the bakery smells and the flowers and the Loire River . . ."

I was also discovering French movies. "Last night we saw Jean-Luc Godard's *La Chinoise*. Also have seen *Belle de Jour*, with Catherine Deneuve. The most fun was afterwards going to a café and feeling entirely in my element."

On my last day in Tours, on October 25, "I took off on my bike to explore and ended up in Amboise, one of the most beautiful Gothic-Renaissance châteaux, built by Charles VIII, where Leonardo lived and is buried. The town itself is charming, built on the Loire and retains its 13th Century appearance. I discovered several tiny villages along the River. In the cool tranquility of the village church I can't help but kneel and pray. I feel someone will hear me say 'thank you.'

"One of my professors invited me for a drink at his home this week. It was one of my best evenings. We had champagne, delicious cake, and what *ambiance!* He and his wife have an old townhouse in Tours full of old books, paintings, and carpets. And one motorcycle the whole family shares! They'd rather spend their money on champagne than cars! What wisdom. They showed me their old family albums and told their tales of the Occupation, the Bombing and how they met each other through the American troops. It's amazing," I wrote my parents, "how much the War is still present in people's lives and memories here. After so many years, they still talk about it, even at the Clouets."

For all my pretense of being a woman of the world, the scribbled lines at the end of my extravagantly enthusiastic account of life in *la douce France* are revealing. "I suddenly had such a pang to have you here with me!" I wrote my mother. "Deep down, I'm still the little girl who needs a hug from Mama twice a day. I miss you so much sometimes. Nobody has a Mother like you. I'm crying now so I'd better stop."

"I can't tell you how excited I am about Paris!" I wrote in my final letter from Tours. "We leave on Saturday morning and will stop on the way at Chartres and arrive in Paris in the afternoon. I am particularly pleased with my housing: I shall be living in the heart of the Latin Quarter, two steps from the Sorbonne, across the street from the Luxembourg Gardens, off the Boulevard Saint Michel: 2 Place Edmond Rostand (how perfect, Papa, since I know Rostand's Cyrano de Bergerac is your favorite)."

I can still recite the poem I memorized that fall, "Ma Bohème," by Arthur Rimbaud, mumbling it like a prayer during solitary rambles along the Loire, and soon the Seine. It was my personal anthem.

Je m'en allais, les poings dans mes
    poches crevées;
Mon paletot aussi devenait idéal;
J'allais sous le ciel, Muse! Et j'étais ton
    féal;
Oh! là là! que d'amours splendides j'ai
    rêvées!

I went off, my fists in my torn pockets
My overcoat too became ideal
I walked beneath the sky, Muse! And I
   was your liege;
Oh what splendid love affairs I dreamed
   of.

I never returned to visit the Clouet family in their ancient *maison particulière* by the cathedral. I picture their son, Benoit, just a few years older than me, wearing his father's well-worn corduroy jacket, with the patched elbows, now summoning his own children on Saturday morning, "Allez, mes enfants!" Let's go kids! he calls out, as his father had. "À la chasse!" To the hunt! I do not need to return. That world is forever preserved for me in amber.

CHAPTER SEVEN

"Alive and exciting at all hours of the day," I wrote in my first letter home from Paris, on October 25, 1967. "I live in a lovely, typical 19th Century Paris Haussmann building, with the usual high ceiling, moldings, marble fireplace, and an unbelievable view of the Luxembourg Gardens. At sunset or in the morning with all the little boys in their silly short pants sailing their boats in the fountain and their mamas shouting, 'Jean-Paul tu vas tomber!' " Fallen chestnuts filled the park's gravel walks. I polished them on my sleeve before pocketing them, as I had as a child in Budapest parks.

In Paris, I felt connected to history in a way I did not in America. Elderly men I passed in the Latin Quarter, with empty sleeves pinned to the shoulder of their jackets, reminded me of the not-so-distant war. Some of them wore their medals pinned to their frayed lapels.

I fell asleep to the roar of motorcycles under my window on place Edmond Rostand and the two-note (high/low) sirens in the distance. I would open my windows the minute I awoke and inhale the blend of diesel from the traffic and coffee from the café Le Rostand below. "Paris s'éveille" (Paris Awakes) was the hit song in those days, and it always seemed to be playing on some distant radio. Even now, listening to that song on my iPod brings back those first Parisian mornings. "Il est cinq heures, Paris s'éveille . . ." "It's five a.m. and Paris awakes . . ."

Late at night, famished, I tiptoed across the creaky parquet toward the kitchen. The minute I crossed the threshold, my landlady, Madame Koumarianos, magically appeared. "Vous n'avez pas dîné, Kati?" she asked, her eyebrows terrifyingly arched. You haven't had dinner, Kati? She was not responsible for my *dîner* and was not about to let me tear off the corner of a stale baguette. But not even this brittle Greek widow could dampen my excitement. "J'ai toujours faim, Madame!" I replied with what I hoped was my most irresistible smile. I am always hungry! It was true. In Paris I was always hungry. All my senses were heightened.

I was living in an enchanted world, which

I tried to capture in my weekly letters to my parents. "The Seine: different at all hours. In the morning I watch the old guys setting up their little stalls of old prints, rare books and even rarer junk. The artists all look their parts, as accurately reproduced by Hollywood. To sit in Notre-Dame after sunset, quiet as a tomb with only candlelight, the stained glass beautiful even in the dark, is eerie and soothing — and overpowering."

In those days, moving to Paris was a real displacement: no phone calls, email, Skype, or any of those other twenty-first-century tools. My letters home were my only means of communication.

By November, I was in love with a fellow student at "Sciences Po," Paris's prestigious Institute of Political Science. Among George's many virtues was that, in addition to his perfect French, this French-Canadian spoke Hungarian. Our parents had been friends in Budapest. "George and I," I wrote home, "are so much alike. We laugh over the same ridiculous things. He is the older brother I always wanted — *et plus encore*." I added that in case they missed the point that I had my first serious boyfriend.

Our twosome was rounded out by another Sciences Po classmate, a violinist studying under the legendary Nadia Boulanger. Bruno Monsaingeon was Parisian to his fingertips and his family more or less adopted me. "I spent all day Sunday with the Monsaingeon family," I gushed to my parents. "They have an amazing apartment, full of books, paintings and such warmth. After lunch, Bruno played the violin and his father — a surgeon — the piano."

Even bad weather was cause for celebration in Paris. "Yesterday it poured rain," I wrote on November 1, "and I went out very early and stood on the Pont Alexandre III and the city was quiet for once, and I could take in the river with Notre-Dame astride it, and the Invalides behind me. I admit to you that this pearly grey landscape so moved me that I cried."

I was discovering art. "It is so much easier to appreciate Utrillo if you have just walked the same streets in Montmartre that he painted . . . I have been camping out at the Louvre as we are having our first big art exam next week. I have to be familiar with everything from Giotto to Corot for this one. I feel almost at home now in that immense palace, I spend so much time there."

Afternoons, I sometimes ducked into one of the Latin Quarter's small movie theaters, where a churchlike hush reigned. The classics of French cinema, from *Hôtel du Nord* to *Jeux Interdits* as well as the films of Jean Renoir and Jean-Luc Godard, entered my life that year. My favorite by far was the haunting *Les Enfants du Paradis*, which I saw a half-dozen times.

And music! "The Orchestre de Paris concert was one of the most movingly beautiful things I have ever heard. I have never heard Beethoven's 5th so powerfully played. And Mozart's concerto for flute played by Jean-Pierre Rampal — magnificent! Music has become so important for me." As usual for me, my sudden passion for music had a romantic source: Bruno, my classmate and companion, transformed from amusing pal to elusive artist and fantasy object when he picked up his violin and began to play. Listening enraptured to his rendition of the *Dumky Trio* by Dvořák, I dreamed about a future of nothing but music and long evenings of clever conversation and laughter. "On Tuesday," I wrote home on March 7, "Bruno gave his annual spring recital — Dvořák, Mozart and Brahms, beautifully and movingly executed. This boy has real genius." I wrote with new authority. "I've learned so much from him about how to listen and love music. I love him too. He has a heart of gold. After his concert we went to his place with several friends — mostly musicians. We made hot wine and talked until morning."

Bruno introduced me to his favorite corner of Paris — now mine. One winter afternoon as we were both leaving Sciences Po, he grabbed my arm and told me to hop on his motorbike — he had a treat for me. I hung on to Bruno as we careened in and out of dark, winding, cobblestoned streets in a neighborhood I did not recognize, and arrived at our destination. We faced a quiet square framed by pink brick pavilions and slate roofs and interconnected with arcades. I was instantly spellbound by the place des Vosges. The harmony of the square, the contrast of the lush green center where children played and lovers sat in the winter half light, framed by the breathtaking architecture, was startling in the dark and dingy Marais. The pavilions' façades were still covered in soot then, before Paris started its great cleanup. Bruno and George and I returned often that year with wine and baguettes, which we consumed on the grass — something you cannot do in most Parisian parks.

Michel de Montaigne was another revelation. In the Sorbonne's Grand Amphithéâtre, a coliseum-size hall, I listened enraptured to a professor I could barely see. Montaigne, he explained, was the first modern man, a real humanist who could teach us a thing or two about how to live our lives. As I was searching for just such a role model, I dove into the *Essays* and began a lifelong relationship with the man and his words. Montaigne called his literary project "essays," meaning "trials," and the word entered the lexicon. I appreciated his absence of certitude and his tolerance of all human foibles — as if they were good things. I was a bookish girl and thus I admired his decision at age thirty-eight to retire from public life to spend more time in his library and writing. Thirty-eight seemed the right age to retire from the world. The fact that the Vatican called Montaigne shameless for embracing his "vices" (meaning his self-absorption) added to his appeal. Let us be kind to *ourselves*, my sixteenth-century hero preached. No one had ever given me that advice. Excel and you will be respected and even loved, was what my parents preached. "We are great fools," Montaigne wrote. " 'He has spent his life in idleness,' we say. 'I have done nothing today.' What? Have you not *lived?* That is not only the most fundamental but the most illustrious of your occupations . . . to compose our character is our duty, not to compose books and to win battles and provinces, but order and tranquility in our conduct. Our great and glorious masterpiece is to live!"

I was not yet interested in Montaigne's views of love and loss as part of the human condition. That would come much later. But I do remember leaning back in a wrought-iron chair, my feet propped up on the stone balustrade overlooking the fountain of the Luxembourg Gardens, a well-thumbed paperback of his *Essays* in my lap. The late-afternoon sun cast a glow on the yellow and orange flower beds, and the leaves of the chestnut trees shimmered gold. I had found the key to happiness.

So besotted was I with my Parisian life that I did not even mind the lack of individual attention from professors. For me it was part of learning to be self-reliant. Of course, I knew I would go home to America in a year or two (I couldn't think of returning after only one year) to a different education system. But for now, on my own for the first time, I was learning who I was, and how I wanted to live.

I had always been a dreamy child. I was astonished at my energy.

"If you are perhaps wondering when I

manage to squeeze in any studying," I wrote home, obviously in answer to my parents' query, "well, I've accustomed myself to going with little sleep — and I still wake up fresh in the morning . . . At 8:15 I set off for either the Louvre (25 mins) or to the Sorbonne (5 mins) or to Sciences Po (15 mins) each morning. My day is filled with classes, studying, walking, going out in the evening (my evening meal is between 9 and 10). I just live on the streets here," I wrote.

One reason I was never "home" was my annoying landlady. I recall that once when I was under the weather, George came over with cold medicine and flowers and was sprawled at the foot of my bed while I was under the covers. Madame Koumarianos burst in and, with a triumphant look of "Aha, I knew it!" exclaimed, "Mais, Kati, je vous croyais une fille bien!" I thought you were a nice girl, Kati.

Since he had a tiny kitchen and was a good cook, most evenings I spent at George's place. I remember every step of my solitary walk home each night around midnight from the rue de Grenelle, crossing the rue de Rennes, to the rue de Vaugirard, up to the Odéon Theater, to the rue de Médicis. Alone, late at night I punched in the code that swung open my building's massive front door, and felt bold and grown-up.

Gradually, I was making discoveries that cast the French in a slightly less flattering light. "In Paris, especially," I wrote home, "they are suspicious of *les étrangers*, very willing to exploit you, and often resentful of Americans — convinced that we are all wealthy. The French lack the spontaneity and the warmth of many Americans. They are often too concerned with '*le comme il faut*' — appearances. The ones that are *sympa*, however, are witty, cultured and charming. It isn't enough to be friendly here to be accepted. You have to contribute something as far as intellect and humor go. It's an entirely different world than the one I left behind, but I feel very much at ease in this one."

The letters, for all their determined sophistication, at times reveal a little girl feeling far from home. "Next year," I wrote my papa, who was planning a skiing trip without me, "you and I can take to the hills together. Oh I can't wait. I miss you so much. It's been so long already."

Rereading these letters for the first time I am struck by my frequent expressions of gratitude. "I can never thank you enough for this amazing chance you have given me,"

I wrote in almost every single letter. "I cannot believe my good fortune to have you as my parents." Yet I was a scholarship student, mostly living on my summer earnings. This was not gratitude typical of an American teenager. It was born of the still fresh memory of the long separation from my parents just a decade before, when they were jailed as American spies and my sister and I were left in the care of strangers in Budapest. As to a phone call home, that was beyond my means.

But my enchantment continued. "Spring arrived to Paris," I wrote home on March 23. "All of a sudden all the cafés moved outside and everybody shed their coats. There are even more than the usual number of amorous couples in the Luxembourg.

"I bumped into Bruno in the afternoon and he said, 'Let's take off for Fontainebleau.' And so we did, along with two French pals. Sunday we went to mass in the village church and had café and croissants with the locals, bought lots of food and cooked a great meal. We hiked all afternoon in the Barbizon forest, went to a local soccer match, listened to Bruno play his violin, made dinner, built a fire and drove back to Paris at 10pm."

Discovering the bargain bins on the rue

St.-Placide, I gradually transformed myself into the facsimile of a chic Parisian girl. Well-cut pants (instead of baggy jeans) and a trench coat became my uniform. And, of course, I learned to tie scarves.

CHAPTER EIGHT

I was studying in the hushed library of Sciences Po, on the rue St.-Guillaume, working on two term papers, one on Proust's moral satire, and another on Rimbaud's fatalism. I heard the low rumble of a demonstration on the nearby boulevard St.-Germain and suddenly realized I was virtually alone. And then abruptly, my enchanted Parisian life exploded in chaos. "This week has brought Revolution to the Quartier Latin," I wrote home on May 10. "For the past couple of nights I've had *gaz lacrymogène* (tear gas) in my eyes, was clubbed as I left the Restaurant Universitaire on the rue Mabillon, by cops who do not differentiate between anybody who attends the Sorbonne, where, by the way, I no longer have classes. I have been locked inside cafés and apartment buildings, where I was forced to take refuge when the battle got overheated. It's my first taste of street violence since Budapest."

Roughly one decade after the revolution that ended my childhood and forced my family to flee, I was caught up in another uprising. This one was not my own. *Les jours de mai*, as it has come to be known, started partly due to those hangar-size classrooms, and distant professors who disappeared immediately after they delivered lectures, unchanged for decades. The spark was lit in the suburban campus of the University of Paris at Nanterre. It seemed such a trivial issue. Boys camping out in the girls' dorms. But the uprising had a fiery leader, Daniel Cohn-Bendit, "Danny le Rouge" (so named for his politics as well as his fiery hair), who brought a few hundred supporters to the Sorbonne to carry on the protest. (It so happened that on the same day, my future husband arrived as the youngest delegate to the Vietnam Peace Conference across the river, at the Élysée Palace. But we would not meet for almost two decades.)

So the uprising moved into my neighborhood. The Grand Amphi, where the week before we were listening to a lecture about Montaigne, became ground zero of the revolution. My first impression was that this was hardly a serious business: all talk and theater, as far as I was concerned. But then the Sorbonne's rector called in the police to clear out the place, and the protests turned violent.

They arrived in buses; the dreaded CRS, Compagnies Républicaines de Sécurité, the riot police, trained for mob busting. Their buses snaked up the Boule Miche and stayed there for weeks, a powerful, menacing sight that transformed the student quarter. We peered inside those big blue buses and observed frightening, extraterrestrial creatures. Their large bodies were padded and ready for combat. Even hunched over their card games, awaiting orders to attack, the CRS appeared menacing — and middle-aged, to my eyes. I could imagine how bored and itching for action they must be in their claustrophobic confinement. When they poured out of their buses, and, with their rubber truncheons swinging, sprang into action, it was hard to get out of their way. That is what happened to me leaving the university cafeteria, and I had sore shoulders for weeks. "*CRS assassin!*" we chanted, even as we dashed into buildings and cafés for cover.

Battle lines were drawn right in front of my building. Place Edmond Rostand, rue

Gay Lussac, and rue Sufflout were rich in paving stones. All night, an army of students dug up those stones and built barricades. It was impossible to sleep. Police cars, ambulances, shouts, and shrill slogans right outside my window touched a deep childhood fear. I could not join in the excitement of my fellow students. To me this was not an adventure but a bad and dangerous memory.

Opening my window the next morning, I was shaken by the sight. The students had turned over cars to block the CRS advance. Small cars were easy to lift and set on fire, especially if you stuffed trash inside. They smoldered for days. The rain, which never seemed to let up that May, gave the whole neighborhood the sodden feel of a war zone. The students had cut down ancient plane trees to reinforce the barricades. Tear gas hung in the air. My eyes itched but I knew enough not to rub them. My beautiful *quartier* was stripped and terrifying.

The sight of the red flags the students brandished as they linked arms and sang the "Internationale" agitated me, bringing back images from my first revolution. At the beginning, the Budapest uprising was like an exuberant parade. In an attempt by the Hungarian authorities to appease mounting prerevolutionary ferment, my parents were released and we were reunited as a family. I was euphoric. The early, hopeful days of the uprising matched my own excitement at having my parents back. But the revolution quickly turned violent — and then hopeless.

Caught up in the swirl of street scuffles between students and police in Paris, I was haunted by memories of Hungarian secret police agents lynched by angry mobs, images of my family's desperate rush to cross the Danube to sanctuary at the American Embassy, one step ahead of Soviet tanks.

With classes canceled, the Sorbonne closed and the action shifted to the Odéon Theater, a few minutes' walk from my apartment. Every wall in the neighborhood was plastered with communist-style posters featuring some ironic wordplay: *Sous les pavés, la plage!* "Under the paving stones, the beaches!" promised one. *Il est interdit, d'interdire*, "It is forbidden to forbid," and so on. Posters of Lenin, Marx, Marcuse, and Mao adorned walls stripped of the Odéon's theater placards. Most shocking to me was a poster of Stalin. Stalin! Did these "revolutionaries" have the faintest notion of Stalin's cruelty? My enthusiasm for this adventure was rapidly evaporating. I wanted my beautiful Paris back.

The tear gas was so thick in my neighborhood that some nights I could not enter my building. My elegant high-vaulted lobby now sheltered injured students, the *quartier*'s new heroes.

The radio no longer played "Paris s'éveille." Instead, an agitated announcer came on with a stream of battle reports. Five hundred people were wounded in street fighting. Soon the whole city was paralyzed: most of the subway lines stopped running, shops in the neighborhood lowered their iron shutters, and even the cafés closed. Trash piled up in front of the great iron gates of Luxembourg Gardens, which were padlocked.

There was no fresh produce, and even cheese — the French staple — disappeared. Madame Koumarianos's wartime experience manifested itself in the varieties of potato dishes she served for lunch. But my landlady seemed somehow satisfied that the outside world now matched her inner gloom. See, Kati, her pursed lips seemed to say, what a bitter thing is life.

With only a few subway lines still running, and the cafés closed, I felt claustrophobic and depressed. It was an exceptionally cold May. I took shelter in the library of Sciences

Po and tried to prepare for my upcoming orals. I could not afford to miss a year's credits. A friend and I decided to hitchhike around France together. Anything was better than being hungry in Paris and breathing the foul, eye-stinging air. But I really wasn't enjoying the picturesque hamlets of Normandy and Alsace-Lorraine. I felt cut off from my parents. There was no mail service. Unlike the Sorbonne "revolutionaries," who could go home in the evening to the safety and warmth of their parents' homes, I was far from home. Also unlike them, I had been frightened before. I had one place to turn for help: the Paris offices of the Associated Press, my father's employer.

Sitting in the AP's office, off the Champs-Élysées, surrounded by a bank of teletypes and shirt-sleeved reporters banging out copy, I felt on familiar ground. I composed the following letter, which a colleague of my father's then teletyped to Papa. Written in Hungarian, the language in which he and I generally communicated, it was dated May 28, 1968.

Dearest Papa,
As you know, France has been turned upside down. It is astonishing how fast a

beautiful city can be destroyed. Nothing works, and, quite frankly, I am depressed and tired. To get away from the barricades and gas bombs, I have been hitchhiking to Deauville and Alsace. I was unable to enjoy these lovely places because this situation is very upsetting to me. It is my first taste of violence since '56.

I can't tell you what my plans are because there are no flights, but I shall certainly return sooner than expected, early July I think.

Please Papa don't worry about me! I am a big girl and intelligent to boot. As soon as you can please send me money and I will hop on a charter. I don't know if I shall stay in Paris for the general strike. It is completely dead. Wherever I go I shall keep in touch. Hope you got my telegram from Colmar. Please trust me. Kati.

How different from my ecstatic reports of just weeks before. My parents had lived through the Nazi and Soviet occupations of Budapest, imprisonment, and revolution and its bloody aftermath, followed by escape to the West. Their younger daughter suddenly caught between barricades and truncheon-wielding riot police must have been a chilling image for them. At the time, frightened as I was, I never thought of what that evoked for them.

Then, on June 6, my morning radio program did not begin with a report on the number of cars burned or students injured in the Latin Quarter. The news was from Los Angeles, and it was shocking: Robert Kennedy, shot in a hotel kitchen, at the start of his run for the White House. I was reeling. Had the world lost its head? Was no place on earth safe? (Across the Seine, my future husband felt Bobby's death even more sharply — and personally. "I was one of those people," Richard wrote Bobby's widow, Ethel, "who were at just the critical moment of decision about their future when JFK was President. I really did enter the government because of him . . . There was hope and then it was gone — and then it returned, and now it seems gone again.")

This act of mindless violence followed on the heels of Martin Luther King's assassination in Memphis just weeks before. The world seemed a dangerous place now. I had no phone so I walked down the eerily quiet boulevard St.-Michel to Bruno's parents' apartment and placed a call home, my first in almost a year. The sound of my mother's

"Katika" reduced me to tears. All my bravado, all my determined self-sufficiency vanished. Suddenly my plans to hitchhike to Italy seemed the ridiculous dreams of another era. I wanted my parents. I wanted to go home.

The next day, I wrote them. "I've just reserved a place on Icelandic Airlines for the 16th of June. It's all set except I'm still waiting for the money which should arrive, now that mail service is back . . . I can't wait to be with you now. The world is too crazy and I'm tired. I spent the day listening to students at the Sorbonne who have little else to do but talk and shout. I cannot recover from the senseless killing of two brave men and need you to reassure me that sanity exists somewhere."

Before leaving, I took my oral exams at Sciences Po. I faced the legendary professor Jean-Baptiste Duroselle in an empty hall. He asked me to discuss the dissolution of the Ottoman Empire after World War I. The great man peered down with a bemused smile at the determined American girl who had been chasing him for weeks to schedule her orals. Perhaps for that reason, he was generous with my final grade. I also turned in my term papers on Proust, Rimbaud, and Montaigne to the Sorbonne. Frightened and homesick I may have been, but no revolution was going to derail my progress.

Charred cars lying on their sides like wounded animals still disfigured my beloved Quartier Latin when I said *au revoir* on a blustery June morning. My final glimpse of Paris en route to Orly Airport was of a cold, gray, battered city. But I knew I would be back.

■ ■ ■ ■

PART III

■ ■ ■ ■

There is never any ending to Paris
and the memory of each person who
has lived in it differs from that of any
other . . . But this is how Paris was
in the early days . . .
— Ernest Hemingway, *A Moveable Feast*

CHAPTER NINE

Ten years later, I am back in Paris. For ten years, school, graduate school, and then work — first in radio, then in local television — had intervened. I had briefly been married to a fellow graduate student at George Washington University, with whom I traveled to Asia. But I was much too young, too immature, and burning with dreams of an adventuresome life and career, to sustain such an early marriage. We divorced amicably a few years later. Inspired by the example of the two young reporters whose fearless enterprise brought down Richard Nixon's presidency, I too became an investigative reporter, working at a local TV station, WCAU-TV in Philadelphia. My beat was the sometimes dangerous intersection of labor and politics. I received death threats and had a warning bullet hole in my red Toyota. But I was young and felt immortal.

For a while, I was the only Philadelphia reporter covering a particularly violent union of roofers, and, as a result, had a request from the legendary *60 Minutes* reporter Mike Wallace for an interview. "Go ahead, Kati," my boss said with a shrug, "but I'll have to take you off the labor beat. Wallace will trap you into saying something compromising. That's what he does." After a sleepless night with my ego dueling with my love of the hard-fought-for beat, I declined the *60 Minutes* interview. Long after I had left local television and moved to New York, Wallace would greet me with "So how is the only woman in America ever to turn me down?"

I worked hard to get the network's attention. I won a George Foster Peabody Award for a special report on the Philadelphia Orchestra's historic trip to China — the first cultural exchange between the two hostile powers. But my triumph was marred by an act that did not yet have a name. The term *sexual harassment* would not be coined until the late seventies. After the New York award ceremonies, instead of heading to Penn Station for the train back to Philadelphia, my boss directed the car to the Hilton hotel on Sixth Avenue, where he had reserved a room for the two of us. It seems incredible now, but in the mid-seventies, though we had the Pill, women were still an exotic and precarious presence in the workplace. This was especially so in the sexist, male province of newsrooms. Terrified of losing my job, I spent the next few hours talking — fast and furiously. Like Scheherazade, I spun amusing stories to divert him. Sometime in the early hours he fell asleep, and I crept out and rushed to catch the train back to Philadelphia. I did not think I would ever get another job in television if I said anything — so I didn't. I waited until the Anita Hill–Clarence Thomas hearings in 1991 to go public with my own story of sexual harassment, in an article I wrote for *Newsweek*.

All the while, I dreamed of the life of the foreign correspondent. The dream of Paris reached back to childhood, and the abrupt end of my student days, which had literally gone up in smoke a decade earlier. In the intervening years, I continued to gobble up paperbacks of Balzac, Stendhal, and Zola, and if a French bistro opened in Washington or Philadelphia, I was among the first to book a table. My personal anthem continued to be the Rimbaud poem I had memorized while biking in the Loire valley.

■ ■ ■ ■

In late 1977, I finally reached the Mount Everest of broadcast journalism. ABC News offered me a job as foreign correspondent and bureau chief in the West German capital, Bonn. I would be living close enough to Paris for it to be a part of my life again.

Before leaving, I went to say good-bye to my parents in Washington. I remember chatting in the kitchen with my mother when Papa poked his head in. "Come, Kati," he said, pulling me toward our den. "Watch this reporter on ABC. He has all the qualities of a great broadcaster: a sense of place, a sense of history, and he speaks well, and he is very handsome. Watch, Kati, and learn from Peter Jennings." I also remember my mother, somewhat later, shaking her head in a way that was almost resigned and, in her wonderful Hungarian-accented English, saying, "I do not think you and he will be *indifferent* to each other."

It is January 1978, my first week as foreign correspondent. En route to assume my post in Bonn, I am spending some weeks in London, learning the ropes of satellite feeds and network operations in ABC's largest overseas bureau. Germany, the front line in the Cold War, was a big story. A breaking story was unfolding there, which made it an even more urgent assignment. A new and violent movement had sprung up in Western Europe: domestic terrorism. Homegrown discontents lashed out against powerful symbols of the postwar German "economic miracle." The Red Army Faction, which had its Italian counterpart, the Red Brigades, gangs of cold-blooded youths, raged against their "bourgeois" elders and set out to rebuff their parents' burdensome Nazi/fascist legacies. Between 1970 and the time I took up my post in January 1978, the Red Army Faction had murdered twenty-eight soldiers, policemen, and corporate leaders: 1977 was their bloodiest year. They kidnapped and executed the CEO of Daimler-Benz, Hanns-Martin Schleyer, before shooting the West German attorney general and soon the president of the Dresdner Bank.

This murderous rampage had led ABC to offer me the German post. I had learned German as a child and had a record as a fearless reporter. Neither the network nor its new hire anticipated that I would fall in love before I even reached my assignment.

I watched the story unfold from London with growing impatience. The image of the glamorous, brave foreign correspondent shimmered in front of me. But the news business was a more leisurely affair in those days. First I had to earn my stripes at ABC's London bureau, a warren of offices on staid Carburton Street. I was duty correspondent in the quiet bureau, recording voiceovers of the war in the Ogaden region of Somalia, an oil spill off the Normandy coast, and the usual troubles in the Holy Land, stories that never went away but did not rate a human presence on the scene. "Wallpaper," in network parlance.

As my first weekend as foreign correspondent approached, Paris — so close — beckoned. From my glass cubicle in the largely empty newsroom, I phoned my sister Juli, living in Paris. "I could get in by late Friday," I told her. "I'm already sick of hotel life," I said, longing for family and the domesticity of Juli's Paris home and new baby.

"And just who do you think is going to cover for you here?" a disembodied voice, passing by my office's open door, growled. "Me?"

"Who is that?" my sister asked. "Sounds rude." Oh, that's Peter Jennings, I answered.

Don't worry, I'll deal with him. See you Friday.

Hanging up, I marched down the hall to the senior foreign correspondent's spacious corner office. Crammed with tribal and war mementos, a colorful kilim on the floor, and a Syrian pearl-inlaid table piled high with books on the Middle East and Africa, it all reminded me I was now in the lair of the man universally known as PJ, or, more derisively, Peter of Arabia. Famous and improbably good-looking. "Hi," I said. "I'm Kati, the new girl. En route to take up my post in Germany. As bureau chief," I said with emphasis.

"I know exactly who you are," Peter answered, barely looking up, "and I also know there are two correspondents in the bureau at the moment. You and me. You are the weekend duty correspondent. Which means if anything breaks, you are on it. Did you think I was going to cover for you while you stroll around Paris?" he said, in one clipped Anglo-Canadian breath. I was reeling. He was a legend. I was the newest and youngest and probably the greenest foreign correspondent on the planet. I mumbled something about how quiet the world seemed and how I hadn't seen my sister in so long and . . . "Okay, well, go ahead," he shrugged. He was almost horizontal in his chair, with his feet propped up on the vast desk. I noticed he was wearing Hush Puppies. Not Gucci loafers. I found this endearing.

"Don't blame me if something breaks," he said, sitting up suddenly and reaching for the phone. My time was up. He was soon chatting to someone he called "Squire." I soon learned that all men were "Squire" and all women "Darling" in Peter's vocabulary. What a total jerk, I mumbled on the way back to my microscopic glass cage. And went off to Paris.

In the taxi heading to my sister's place on rue Chardon-Lagache, in the sixteenth arrondissement, I could hardly believe my good fortune. I was back — and not as a tourist but as a bureau chief for ABC News. Paris preened for me on this crisp winter day. It was heaven to breathe that pungent air — already tinged with the smell of hot chestnuts — and bliss to descend with my sister and her baby into the familiar Métro, its map still engraved in my memory like a poem. We tore by those stations named for historic battles — Solférino, Austerlitz, Stalingrad (but not Waterloo!) — that always unleashed my imagination. At the outdoor market in Passy, Juli and I shopped for cheese and fruits, before moving on to the splendors of the charcuterie. Pushing Mathieu's stroller, I began to relax for the first time since I arrived in London to begin my new life. Paris was mine again.

At my sister's place, unloading our string shopping bags in her kitchen, the telephone rang. It was Bill Milldyke, the London bureau manager. "Kati, there's been an IRA attack in Belfast." For just a second, I couldn't remember where Belfast was. "You've got to get there, ASAP," he went on. "It's a dog show. People and dogs injured. You'll make the evening news. Best you fly to Dublin. Then make your way to Belfast from there." He sounded like he was speaking to an actual foreign correspondent for whom getting from Paris to Dublin, and thence to Belfast, was like taking the D.C.–New York shuttle. "Okay, Bill. I'll upcome from there, when I get in," I said, recalling that everybody at the network was always "upcoming" from someplace.

With my sister's help, I caught a plane to Dublin that afternoon. It was dark when I hauled my bag toward the car rental place for my onward journey into Northern Ireland and the war zone. A large, smiling man intercepted me with a hearty "You must be Kati, if I'm not mistaken?" His name was Johnny and he was the local Irish "fixer," one of the network's unsung heroes who made the wheels go around for ignorant arrivals from New York like me. "Peter called me and told me to meet you here. I'll try to make things easy for you. Let's go and get you to Belfast without getting either of us killed on the road." During that dark and anxious journey across No Man's Land, Johnny spoke with warmth about Peter. "One of the great reporters," he said. "And a good man, too."

I checked into Belfast's fortresslike Hotel Europa. ("Now, miss, when the bombs fall, you follow these steps down to the cellar," the bellman explained, taking my suitcase.) Waiting for me in the lobby was a tall, elegant man and his much shorter partner. "I'm Nicholas," the tall man said with a faint, non-Irish accent. It turned out he was a Russian aristocrat and a legendary cameraman in the field. "This is Didi, your soundman," he said, pointing toward a balding man who flashed a tobacco-stained smile my way. Didi was German and lit up his next cigarette while the one he was working on was still going. "Peter called me," Nicholas said as we hopped in his van. "Not to vorry. Ve shoot beautiful pictures.

You make big story. I make you star."

And so we did. On a weekend news show when not much was going on at home, a dog show in Belfast, with more canine than human loss of life, got more time than I deserved. Thanks to Johnny and Nicholas and Didi we navigated Belfast's No Man's Land. I interviewed masked gunmen I would later meet without their masks, in suits and ties, at the Council on Foreign Relations.

I returned to London exhilarated. I had passed my first test. Marching into Peter's corner office with hand extended, I thanked him. "That's okay," he said. "Let's start again." He asked me if I liked Gilbert and Sullivan. I lied and said, "Sure. But here is the problem. British Airways lost my bag in Belfast. I have only the clothes on my back. The rest I had already shipped to Germany." Peter seemed to have solutions for any problem a foreign correspondent might encounter. "Tell Milldyke you need an advance. Then go to Harrods. Buy yourself a couple of nice things. You'll need some tweeds, soft wool things. It gets cold here." I could feel him quickly and critically appraising my very untweedy American outfit. "You'd look good in a kilt, too." So began my makeover. Later, I wondered if he had something to do with British Air losing my bag.

Wearing my new heather gray suit (with a skirt, as I had noticed Peter noticing my legs), I waited for him to finish the live evening newscast. Off we went to Gilbert and Sullivan. Only it turned out he had picked the wrong night and instead of *H.M.S. Pinafore*, we were suddenly watching a modern dance company from Marseilles. Not knowing each other's taste, we sat quietly through the first act. At intermission we both admitted a total lack of interest in the performance. "Let's get out of here," he said. "I'll take you to my favorite place for dinner." It was Bentley's on Swallow Street, off Regent Street. We ate oysters and drank Montrachet and Bentley's became our place. I think we were in love before the check arrived. He walked me home to the Hotel Montblanc near Marble Arch. He kissed me good night — a chaste kiss on the cheek. The next night we returned to Bentley's (Peter was a creature of habit) and after a few glasses of wine, he said we would produce beautiful and smart children together. This wild notion — on our second evening together — carried a serious undercurrent, which we both understood.

And so began a passionate and tormented

love story that lasted fifteen years. Those children we talked about are now grown and wiser than their elders, when they joked about having them, during their second dinner at Bentley's.

CHAPTER TEN

The seventies were a dispirited age, an unheroic time. I looked back on the thrilling sixties and the Age of Aquarius as a dim memory of discovery, of great music, of first love, and of Paris. Now East and West, Washington and Moscow, were frozen in a sullen state of neither war nor peace, which we assumed would be permanent. Gray, geriatric leaders in the Kremlin faced an untried and uncharismatic president in the White House. I was assigned to cover the front line of the same war whose most treacherous face I had witnessed as a little girl in Budapest.

Bonn in those days was not much changed from John le Carré's description of a decade earlier in his classic Cold War thriller, *A Small Town in Germany*. "Bonn was a Balkan city, stained and secret, drawn over with tramwire. Bonn was a dark house where someone had died, a house draped in Catholic black and guarded by policemen. Their leather coats glistened in the lamplight, the black flags hung over them like birds. Now a car, now a pedestrian hurried past, and the silence followed like a wake . . . A tram sounded but far away."

I arrived in the once-sleepy German capital to find it in a virtual state of siege. (With Berlin deep in the Soviet zone, Bonn was chosen partly for its proximity to the home of Chancellor Konrad Adenauer, the first president of the Federal Republic.) Two and a half decades after the end of World War II, Bonn bristled with submachine-gun-toting, green-uniformed security forces, stopping cars and asking to see "Papieren, bitte." An old movie, rewound again. German authorities had reason for alarm. Their homegrown terrorists were skilled political murderers and were bent on provoking the state into overreaction.

Still, it was exciting to move into my new apartment in the pretty, provincial German city on the Rhine, and to take charge of the ABC Bureau, in the golden age of foreign corresponding. In Pressehaus II, an easy walk to the Bundestag, the parliament of the Federal Republic of Germany, my office was wedged between the *New York Times* and the *Los Angeles Times* bureaus. I was

103

taking my place among the Big Boys, for indeed, the press corps was virtually all male.

Peter arrived during my first weekend, and missed very few after that. Zipping down the Bonn–Cologne autobahn to the airport early Saturday morning in my green Volkswagen Beetle to pick him up became part of my routine — and the high point of my week. He always brought a gift. A piece of Wedgwood from London, or more exotic items if he'd been traveling that week. One Saturday he arrived with a richly embroidered Palestinian dress, which I wore all weekend.

We lived quietly and domestically. We shopped together in Bonn's picturesque outdoor market and cooked in my tiny, sunny kitchen. We walked and biked along the Rhine, and planned our future. Bonn was a fine place for two people in love, uninterested in nightlife or the company of anyone but each other. In some ways Peter was more eager for a settled life than I — the freshly minted foreign correspondent. There was never any doubt that we would spend our lives together. It was just a question of when. Before fame, before stratospheric success, and even before children, we lived our best days in that small town in

Germany.

Peter trained me to keep one ear cocked to the clickety-clack of the wires bringing news from other ABC bureaus and the world, to be prepared for the call from the assignment desk. He tutored me in the ways of the network news hierarchy: the anchor's droit de seigneur always trumped the local correspondent, a mere serf, when a Lord or Lady of the Realm was visiting.

Soon I learned this lesson the hard way. Barbara Walters arrived on July 15, 1978, to cover a story I had been working on for weeks: President Jimmy Carter's first state visit to the Federal Republic of Germany on the occasion of the economic summit. I returned to my office after lunch one afternoon to find the Grande Dame of television news occupying my desk, perusing my scripts. "Nice work," she said, barely looking up. "We can use these on *GMA* [*Good Morning America*]." I understood that the *we* was royal.

I retreated from my office, in tears. Peter followed me. "She used to do it to me, too," he said, an arm around my slumped shoulders. "Forget it. When she leaves town, you get your story back." What he didn't say was that he had the same rights and privileges as "Bigfoot" local correspondents himself.

When the Bigfeet departed, I moved to covering stories from the twilight atmosphere of the divided city of Berlin. I reported on the unmasking of former West German chancellor Willy Brandt's personal aide, Günter Guillaume, as an officer in the East German secret police. Le Carré could not have improved on this scenario.

Standing in front of the hideous concrete barrier that sliced the real German capital in two, I spoke into the ABC News camera: "The Berlin Wall is the most cruel symbol of a divided Germany. The biggest new spy threat is considered to be from the thousands of women, who work at all levels of the government in the West German capital of Bonn. Given the loneliness of that one-business town, women are often vulnerable to the advances of professional spy recruiters." The camera then followed me into a Berlin prison, where I interviewed a "secretary spy," Renate Lutze, who had been seduced and recruited by Brandt's aide.

From my perch at the Hotel Kempinski, on the glittering Kurfürstendamm, I dictated my scripts to New York, as my parents had from our Budapest apartment. Meanwhile, Peter kept my parents apprised of my progress from London. His weekly phone calls were a cherished ritual for my mother and father.

But as my love affair with Peter deepened, spy swaps, airline hijackings, and political kidnappings no longer made my pulse race quite as fast. Would I be back from Amman, Mogadishu, Rome, or Brussels by the weekend? The need to be with Peter was now edging out my zeal to "make air" on *World News Tonight*. But not quite. The dilemma was how to balance the two. For Peter it was no dilemma at all. He was the star and he could do as he pleased. The dreaded New York assignment desk could only *suggest* stories to him. But they really didn't need to. He was the consummate pro who could smell a story from several time zones away and rarely missed one.

"The Desk" was the bane of my life. They called at all hours. ("What time is it there?" was the most irritating question asked by assignment editors calling at 3 A.M. and pretending not to know.) How fast can you get to Moscow or Athens, was all they needed to say to me. The rest was up to me. A part of me was still thrilled to pack and go, but now there was another part of me.

I did reckless things just to be with him. Once, while filming at a Palestinian refugee camp outside Amman, I hired a Jordanian taxi, and, for a king's ransom, had him drive me to Jerusalem, where Peter was on assignment. I will never forget the look on his face when I surprised him at the American Colony Hotel. "Aren't you supposed to be in Amman?" Peter gasped. "Well, yeah, but it's such a short drive — less than an hour — and here you were, and there I was, and we can have dinner together, and I'll be back in Amman before anyone finds out." The *distance* was not the problem — people commute farther in New York. But this was the Middle East, where distance is measured not in miles but in geopolitics. Amman and Jerusalem might as well have been on different continents. "How do you think you'll get back to Jordan from Israel?" the seasoned Mideast veteran asked his greenhorn girlfriend. It turned out there was no return trip from Jerusalem to Amman, by taxi or camel. I had to fly to Paris and from there to Amman, at great personal expense, and in a total panic that my dinner in Jerusalem would register on the radar of the ever-suspicious assignment desk.

Paris was where we lived the most romantic and melodramatic part of our love story. This was not the Paris of my Left Bank student days. Our Paris was the opulent Right Bank, the Champs-Élysées and the rue du Faubourg St.-Honoré, with the Tuileries replacing the Luxembourg Gardens as our park. No more creaky parquet or Madame Koumarianos's booby-trapped kitchen door. The ABC Bureau on tree-lined avenue d'Eylau was presided over by the former Kennedy White House spokesman Pierre Salinger. Our offices reeked of Pierre's cigar. Peter chain-smoked Player's cigarettes, sometimes lighting one and then leaving it in the ashtray to burn while he left the room. There was always a hot lunch prepared by the bureau's chef waiting for visiting firemen. Peter and I preferred Chez Francis, on nearby place d'Alma. ABC once photographed us lunching there for an ad campaign. Peter, the dashing, trench-coated foreign correspondent sucking on a pipe, me in my chic Parisian suit.

There was an almost unbearable intensity to our romance, as one of us was always just arriving, or just leaving. After Peter finished his live "stand-upper" on the Champs-Élysées, we would walk over to Fouquet's. Sitting in the sidewalk café of the world's showiest boulevard with Peter and Pierre, sipping Kirs, I felt like I was in one of those black-and-white films I used to watch in my student afternoons in the Latin Quarter. I could hardly believe that this handsome, famous man was in love with me. I marveled at the grace with which he moved through crowds, perfectly aware of the impression he was making. The way his immaculately tailored jacket molded to his strong chest, with his long legs under the table entwined with mine — who cared if I arrived exhausted the next day in Berlin or Vienna?

We always stayed at the Lancaster Hotel on the rue de Berri. The concierge, in cutaways the Duke of Windsor would admire, became the coconspirator of our love affair. He called me "Mademoiselle Incognito," as we were still not quite open about our relationship. Peter was separated but not yet divorced. His former lovers were legion. One of them ran the Paris bureau and was implacably sullen toward me. When a group of South Moluccan independence fighters seized a railway car with Dutch passengers, Renate instructed me to make my way to this remote corner of the Netherlands *tout de suite*. "A camera crew will meet you there," she said, with few other guidelines. "Just rent a car and here's a map." It was my first time driving long-distance in Europe and it took me days. But she got me out of Paris and away from Peter.

En route back to Paris, I wrote Peter, "I

yearn for that headstrong, untiringly ambitious refugee girl who wanted it all. The American Dream. She — that lost forever child — had her moments of emotional need — but she never lost sight of what was most important: Her Ambition. Then you came along and it was really like being at square one in the construction of my vision of happiness. It all centers around you now: my need to make you happy, my hunger for permanence with you. All the rest seems trivial now. Stuff I can work out somehow." Rereading this, it's heartbreakingly clear I was trying to persuade myself of something I did not absolutely believe — even then. I was torn between my passion for Peter and my drive to become a great foreign correspondent. That ambition struck Peter as unseemly, *unfeminine*. When he used the word *ambition* as it applied to me he gave it a biting sound, like *avarice*. Indeed there weren't many role models for what I wanted: a big career and a family. I felt there was something wrong with me for wanting both as much as I did. There was no one I could talk to about this, least of all Peter.

"I am drawn to you," I wrote later that spring. "Like Pooh to his pot of honey. Only when you retreat to that defensive cold place — when you imagine something that

111

I swear to you does not exist — only then do *I* want to retreat. Please don't let me!"

Soon my parents arrived in Paris to visit my sister and me, and meet the man Papa had advised me to learn from. We dined on oysters at Peter's favorite restaurant, Prunier, and everybody was delighted by everybody else. As I surveyed that elegant dinner table — my parents, my brother, sister, and French brother-in-law, and Peter, entertaining them with his exploits, as though they were already his family — I beamed with pride. I shot my father a look that said, "See, Papa, I listened to you."

En route to Athens, on Olympic Airlines stationery I wrote Peter, "Thank you for one of my life's most fulfilled weekends. You were wonderful with my family. They took to you instantly . . . I only hope I win your family over just as fast."

From the earliest days the strains of a love affair between two emotionally needy and ambitious people were apparent. Nor did *New York* appreciate its star anchor, being groomed by ABC News president Roone Arledge for big things, crisscrossing Europe and the Middle East chasing its bright new recruit. There was little they could do to Peter. But their power over me was almost

112

infinite.

Before long, my boss, *World News Tonight* producer Av Westin, summoned me home for "a little talk." We met for lunch at the Café des Artistes, the elegant Upper West Side restaurant preferred by ABC executives. Terrified, I faced the smooth Westin and his sidekick, Stan Opotowsky. The head of news operations, Stan was a pudgy, bald, perpetually disheveled figure for whom the term *ink-stained wretch* must have been coined. In the years I knew him I don't think he ever changed his gray shirt, which, I assume, had once been white. He did not like Peter and now he did not like me.

"We had high hopes for you," Av began, with a deep sigh. My blood ran cold. Facing these two men who held my future in their hands, I felt very alone. In that gleaming restaurant, my cherished dreams were evaporating. "You're blowing it, Kati," Av concluded. Stan said nothing, just sat there, his face a grim reprimand.

"What are you talking about, Av?" I asked, for I wasn't going down without a fight. "Have I missed a single story? Have I not done a good job on every single assignment?" "It's not that," Av said, shaking his head. "It's the *perception* people have . . ."

"Perception of what?" I asked, my composure about to slip. "Well," he answered with a deep sigh, "that you are not serious about your job. Because of Peter."

So that was it. No dereliction of duty, just the *perception* of something. I had become water cooler fodder.

"Av," I pleaded. "I love my job. I worked very hard to get here. Let me go back and do my job. I won't let you down. And Peter and I are not a *thing*. We are serious. We love each other." Av kind of snorted and gave me a look that said, "Oh, you poor kid. Are you ever in for it." Stan said nothing.

The lunch was over and I received a stay of execution. Now, so many years later, I flip through my news scripts from those two years as foreign correspondent and I marvel at the range of subjects I covered. Brezhnev in Germany, Jimmy Carter in Germany, the crisis of the neutron bomb, Palestinian refugee camps, terrorist kidnappings, spies in Berlin, civil war in Rhodesia — soon to be Zimbabwe — NATO war games, the Vienna Boys Choir, Fashion Week in Milan, and scores of others. I was a proficient reporter. But my bosses worried about my "perception" problem. Their star reporter and I were conducting a passionate love affair and that was not part of their plan.

114

■ ■ ■ ■

I flew back to Bonn, to my work and to my love — determined to succeed at both. The two were proving increasingly less compatible. I seemed to be forever letting Peter down, and pleading for forgiveness. During the week, I wasn't with him. I was traveling with mostly male camera crews, working with male producers. Peter, used to his girlfriends/wives waiting for him at home, was not happy about this. If, in a feeble attempt to keep my personal and professional lives a millimeter apart, I followed my (mostly male) producer's advice, he took it personally. "I've been in this business a hell of a lot longer than that guy," he would say. "You're going with *his* word?" Few producers enjoyed being in that position. Working with me was becoming hard duty. On May 31, this time on blue Lufthansa stationery, I wrote to Peter: "I felt such agitation in your voice all day. I'm so plugged in to whatever you are thinking, feeling and suppressing that I've shared that agitation all day. I have never before depended on another human being for so much of my own emotional and physical well-being. When you said that I had let you down — the world suddenly

115

went to black. The very last thing I ever, ever want, is to let you down."

Reading this now I wonder what happened to the feisty girl who a decade earlier had written home from the same city, "I am just overflowing with experiences and feelings that I want to share with you! I am savoring every instant to its fullest. Today is my first real day as a scholar at the Sorbonne. I am so excited to take my place in one of those huge amphitheaters and soak up the wisdom of great minds."

Our love story, played out against the backdrop of world events, was never anything but a high-wire act. I had my dream job and I was loved by one of the world's most dashing men. I was leading such an exciting life I brushed off warning signs.

Was it my thirtieth birthday when I realized that maybe I was fooling myself, that possibly beneath its glossy surface, my life wasn't making me happy? We were in Paris, and Peter had arranged a surprise birthday celebration for me. We dined at Maxim's, where a chilled magnum of Dom Perignon, compliments of Pierre Salinger, awaited us at our table. Afterward, Peter took me to the city's most fashionable cabaret, the Crazy Horse. I recall sitting in the front row and gazing at the perfect, cantaloupe-shaped orbs of the dancers' bottoms, swiveling in front of me. Suddenly, I was swept by an inexplicable sadness. Tears started flowing, but I dared not move. Later, peering in the mirror, I felt as if I were looking at a deranged stranger. Was I mourning the end of my youth? But everything was ahead of me! Marriage, children, a brilliant life — exceeding all my fantasies!

So what was the problem here? I had no answer, and did not spend time searching for one. We were passionately in love. We would work things out. His bouts of jealousy were proof of his love for me, I told myself. He was possessive because he adored me. I, the insecure refugee girl, yearned for the sort of uncompromising love he offered. But at times the price seemed too high. When Peter retreated inside an icy shell of hurt and disappointment, which neither humor nor charm nor tears could coax him out of, I was miserable. At such times, there was nothing I could say to reassure him of my love.

My letters to Peter reveal agonizing highs and lows. "Everything seems eminently solvable this morning," I wrote to him in Lebanon. "I mean everything that counts. Not minor problems — like the fighting along the Litani, and four hundred miles of oil spilled off the coast of Brittany — but you and me. I know I won't always feel this patient when you're in a Lebanese ghost town and I'm in London, Bonn, Monrovia — wherever. Your daffodils are still alive, though your tulips look sad."

A month later, he too had been called back to New York. ABC News wanted to entice him to a bigger job. I didn't think we were ready. "From Somewhere Between Berlin and Bonn" I wrote him, "I really feel like we belong in Europe now. New York and Washington seem almost foreign places. I think it's because Europe is where you and I happened . . . Everything I do now is with Us in mind. When I'm writing a script, it's not for ABC's millions (hopefully) of viewers. It's for you. When I dive into a pool, and swim twenty laps fast — it's so I'll be healthy and strong — for you. It's an absolutely new and wonderful way to feel. Five days is my outside limit without you." Peter turned down Roone Arledge's offer of a job in New York.

Then, in late May, despite precautions, I was pregnant. We both wanted desperately to have a child. We were in love and committed to each other, but I knew it was too

118

soon. I had just persuaded ABC of my dedication to my job. I was working hard to prove to the network I could handle my job and my relationship with their star reporter. Abortions were illegal in Germany, so I asked my sister to help arrange one in Paris. Peter met me at the private clinic in the sixteenth arrondissement. He was sad and sweet and held my hand during the procedure. The doctor said I could not fly in a drugged state, so I went without anesthesia. I wanted to be back in Bonn before *New York* noticed my absence. In Bonn, I was alone, and the pain was excruciating. I was depressed for some time, and determined that I would not repeat the experience. But no one at ABC ever found out.

Our bosses did their best to send me on assignments where Peter could not follow me, but he generally showed up anyway, if even for just one night.

My moment of broadcasting glory was to be when I was assigned a multipart report called "Budapest Revisited," the first network report from that dateline since Soviet tanks rolled in 1956.

From on board my Budapest-bound flight, I wrote Peter, "The slow acculturation has begun. The plane is filled with the strange yet familiar sounds of my childhood. Hungarian babies gurgle differently, their mothers comfort them in a tone that is strange to American ears — yet it is all so familiar to me. At the airport in Frankfurt, I had a sudden moment of panic: Why am I doing this alone? You are so far . . . In front of me sits a pretty, red-haired Hungarian woman traveling with two very small children. Does she miss their father as much as I miss you this moment? I envy her. I have only my typewriter in the seat next to mine."

I landed in the city I had fled as a frightened child who had only recently been reunited with her jailed parents.

Two decades later, Budapest seemed eerily unchanged. Wrapped in the dark night of Cold War Eastern Europe, only a few pale neon signs broke the perfect gloom of Budapest at night. A red star still glowed atop the parliament building, Europe's largest, and one of the emptiest. I was bombarded by powerful memories of waking up to find my father gone, of my mother grabbing my sister and me by the hand, to begin a futile search for the man all three of us called Papa. Memories of fear and abandonment crashed just beneath the surface, as I craned my neck out the rickety taxi window en route to my Budapest hotel.

"Let's go by Csaba Utca first," I directed

my taxi driver, up to our old house in Buda. Jumping out of the car, I sprinted up the stairs to the house from where my parents had been taken and from where we began our journey to America. In an instant, the intervening years melted away. I was again the little girl suddenly alone, with only my sister, crying on the curb, where the taxi now waited. My head was spinning with memories, and with unexplored emotions. Nostalgia for my broken childhood, sadness that I was alone for this important trip, and pride, too. I was back in the place that tried to destroy my family, not as a tourist, but representing an American television network.

I did not get a chance to unpack that night. "How fast can you get to Cracow?" the night editor from the New York assignment desk demanded once I reached the Hilton. White smoke above the Sistine Chapel in Rome had just signaled the election of a new pope. His name was Karol Wojtyla, a fifty-eight-year-old Pole, a former archbishop of Cracow. As a Hungarian, a child of the Cold War, raised as a Roman Catholic, I understood this was a momentous, history-making event. The Vatican had outfoxed Leonid Brezhnev's shaky gerontocracy! But to leave Budapest after such a brief glimpse, and after so many years, was emotionally wrenching.

So began my long journey from Budapest to Cracow by plane, train, and car. I arrived the next morning and sent this telegram to room 428–429 in the Hotel Excelsior in Rome. "Dearest Love, Just arrived Cracow. It is dawn. I love you." Unfortunately, the new Holy Father had already left for Rome. Pushing on to his hometown of Wadowice, I was determined to find a story. What I found was a town in the throes of euphoria — literally dancing in its cobblestoned streets. No one had anticipated this bold papal pick. I scored an exclusive interview with the pope's housekeeper, Maria, who had just received a call from the pontiff inviting her to attend his induction in Rome. My crew and I flew there with her, filming her emotional journey, culminating in her reunion with the new pope.

"I thought Kati's Cracow story was very good," Papa wrote Peter, "and both she and her pictures were superior to NBC's. I always was and remain — as she knows — a harsh critic of the family's performances. I wonder whether she and crew will be able to go back to Hungary? The story in Cracow, as far as I can judge is over and tomorrow is the anniversary of the Revolution.

There *should* be a story: perhaps nothing more than the memories of someone who was there as a child."

But instead of Budapest, the network rewarded my enterprise by keeping me in Rome to cover the papal induction. We were about to learn that this pontiff, in answer to Stalin's long-ago taunt, had plenty of divisions behind him. John Paul II, as he called himself, was, by papal standards, a young, vigorous, and charismatic leader who would represent a very real challenge to the Soviet monolith. A great story.

Best of all, Peter was already there. By day we worked side by side, and by night we gorged on spaghetti *alle vongole* and *caprese* salads at Peter's favorite Trastevere trattoria, Piperno. My father wrote Peter and me on September 13, 1978, "Your Rome coverage was superb." Striding out the Excelsior's polished revolving door to the Via Veneto on those late summer mornings, with my camera crew waiting to begin another day's work, and with Peter after work, was exhilarating. Life, for once, seemed balanced.

My mother wrote Peter on October 22, 1978, "My heart always beats faster when I hear you announce 'Kati Marton reporting from . . .' I can't get used to the thrill of it."

ABC did send me back to Budapest later that year. On three consecutive nights on *World News Tonight*, I did my best work yet for the network. It was easy. This was my story. It did not then occur to me that, for my parents, watching me reporting from the country that had jailed them for the same "crime" must have been a freighted moment.

Walking along the Danube, I knew my every step was followed, as my parents' had been. Budapest was then still a city of peeling plaster and crumbling stucco, broken here and there by a few grimy neon signs of a garish blue — but it was still my hometown.

Meeting my childhood friends, I was surprised to learn they had reported our rendezvous to their bosses. That was the law of the People's Republic of Hungary. But the Ice Age of Soviet rule — imposed by weapons and terror — was cracking. I filmed a Hungarian folk festival. A decade earlier, this sort of flamboyant Magyar patriotism would have been considered subversive anti-Soviet nationalism. I danced to a Hungarian rock 'n' roll band in a smoky subterranean nightclub with old friends who still whispered when they spoke of their dreams of travel in the West. They had never left this city and they remembered everything. We stayed up until dawn, laughed at memories of our games, our deaf piano teacher, the drama of my parents' arrest, and the weeks that transformed all our lives: the Hungarian Uprising. They had followed every step of my family's escape and journey to the United States. They had more time and a more intense interest in me than my American friends did.

Strolling on Vaci Street — the Madison Avenue of Budapest — I found the dressmaker who in the fifties had kept my mother in the latest Western fashions. She was still in business. "Katika!" she shrieked when I stepped into her old shop. My reincarnation as an American melted away under her gaze. I was again the earnest, insecure child of parents the state deemed Enemies of the People.

My reporting captured some of the emotions I was feeling. New York showered me with "herograms" for my work. "First rate reporting," anchorman Frank Reynolds wrote in a telegram. "All in New York and Washington bureaus send congratulations. Your father and mother receiving calls from all over the country. Come see them and us soon."

I was exultant on so many levels. I had again demonstrated my value to the network. And I had reconnected with my childhood. Budapest, the city of my deepest fears and longing, was mine again. I had shattered the taboo on the past.

Typically, my father made light of the emotional content of my trip. "Dear Peter," Papa wrote. "First, many thanks for your telephone reports about Kati's meanderings on the other side of the Curtain. Needless to tell you how much they mean to us."

As I left the scene of my triumph, I was preoccupied by Peter. He had filled my Budapest hotel room with roses and long, loving, encouraging telexes. But he sensed I had experienced a powerful personal journey — one from which he felt excluded. "At the end of a week rich and full," I wrote him on November 14, "in a state of agony at your words — I know under the influence of temper and anger — they still ring in my ear. Oh God, I never want to stir such feelings in you. Of course I'm interested in sharing, and in showing vulnerability and need. Am I so bad at all that?"

I tried to pitch myself into my next big story: the delicate process of Germans confronting their own history. Astonishingly, the country's first mass exposure to the Holocaust came with the broadcast of an American television series of the same name. In the breathless style of television news, I reported on ABC: "It has been nothing short of a thunderbolt. The reaction of sixty-five million West Germans confronting their history's most painful chapter for the first time. Incredibly, this national soul-searching has been triggered by an American TV series, seen by twenty million Germans — accomplished what scores of well-meaning documentaries have failed to do: provoked a long-overdue national debate about the past . . . Shock, bewilderment and surprise. Those were the immediate reactions of Germans as they watched the horrors of the Nazi rise to power . . . in their living rooms.

"I sat with a German family and experienced with them the emotional catharsis repeated all over this country. The Knies family of Bonn decided to watch *Holocaust* as a family, all eight members gathered in front of their television sets for seven grueling hours. Willem Knies, once a pilot in Hitler's Luftwaffe, could only say he was seeing nothing he did not already know, but knowing the facts is one thing, experiencing the emotions is another. 'It's terrible,' he said, 'and it's true.'

"Shortly after the broadcast of *Holocaust*," I reported, "West German police started cracking down on bands of neo-Nazis. They've confiscated pictures of Adolf Hitler, swastikas, and even more chilling, an arsenal of machine guns and revolvers and explosives found in a small town near Hanover, where a group of eighteen youths had formed a neo-Nazi training camp.

"But a far greater danger until now had been an unwillingness on the part of most Germans to even admit to the Nazi past . . . In a way this is a period of testing: a nation still on probation in the eyes of much of the world has been on trial in recent weeks — maybe years. Foreign observers, this reporter included, have been astonished at the overwhelming reaction to the broadcast of *Holocaust*. As one German friend put it, 'I don't feel personal guilt for all those things I had nothing to do with. What I do feel now is shame.' . . . This is Kati Marton, ABC News, Bonn."

Again, it was in Paris that Peter and I reunited. The unlikely figure of the brooding religious leader who was about to shake the world to its core brought us together in the French capital. The Grand Ayatollah Khomeini, exiled spiritual leader of Iranian Shiites, slipped into France in late 1978. Following his thirteen-year exile in Iraq, he arrived in the sleepy Parisian suburb of Neauphle-le-Château. Twenty-five miles east of Paris, this leafy hamlet was a strange spot from which to organize a revolution. But that is precisely what the Iranian religious leader planned: the overthrow of Shah Mohammad Reza Pahlavi and the establishment of the Islamic Republic of Iran.

I was thrilled to be assigned to cover Khomeini's French exile. Each morning that winter of 1979, my crew and I drove to the ayatollah's compound. His followers had pitched a huge blue and white prayer tent, which they called a mosque. Khomeini stayed in his modest bungalow, inaccessible to the growing number of us reporters. Our goal was to catch him twice a day as he shuffled from the bungalow to the tent with our cameras and microphones. "Allahu Akhbar!" his supporters shouted when Khomeini appeared. *God is great.* They surged toward the turbaned old man, eager to touch the hem of his black robe. I was chilled by his gaze. His eyes were pitch-black, and beneath his bushy brows they glowered at everyone — his adoring followers included. There seemed no life in his eyes at all. He seemed as repelled by his supporters as by the rest of us. He literally recoiled from being touched by human hands.

One day, I was doing my rapid-fire stand-up report, in time to have the ayatollah in the shot behind me as he crossed the lawn to his tent. Suddenly, I noticed that my cameraman, Tony Hirashiki, had stopped shooting. He seemed frozen in place. "C'mon, c'mon!" I barked, "we haven't got much time." Tony shook his head. I turned around and there, standing behind me, dark and menacing, was the ayatollah himself. Eyes stormier than ever, he gestured with his hands that I should cover my head. I think I was more annoyed than frightened. In those days, Ayatollah Khomeini seemed just an angry old man. The world had not yet encountered his ruthless power. I borrowed a headscarf from a colleague and finished my stand-upper without Khomeini in the shot.

I was not the only one who underestimated Khomeini and what he stood for. The idea that religion would be the most dangerous political force of the late twentieth century seemed inconceivable then. Washington was caught as flat-footed as the rest of us when the ayatollah unleashed his vengeful theocracy a few months later.

Though a sign on the wall of his bungalow informed us that "the ayatollah has no spokesman," we knew better. Sadegh Ghotbzadeh was a dapper Georgetown University School of Foreign Service graduate who befriended all of us in the press corps and acted as Khomeini's emissary. He was charming, flirtatious, and absolutely devoted to his master. The ayatollah referred to Sadegh as "almost my son." Peter and I met Sadegh at his favorite Parisian brasserie, La Closerie des Lilas, dear to both Hemingway and to my father. He and Peter wore almost identical blue blazers. Peter teased Sadegh that he would have made a great foreign correspondent. But Ghotbzadeh had grander dreams.

From a redbrick garage attached to Khomeini's modest house, Ghotbzadeh and other aides, assisted by student volunteers, made cassette tapes of the ayatollah's speeches. Transmitted by telephone to Iranian mosques, Khomeini's noontime sermons in Neauphle-le-Château were heard by millions of Iranians. Sadegh and his cohorts were laying the groundwork for Khomeini's return to his homeland.

On January 16, 1979, I scored a small

scoop. It was the day Mohammad Reza Pahlavi, the once all-powerful Shah of Shahs, who had ruled Iran with an iron fist, fled his country, to begin exile in Egypt. I cornered the shah's son-in-law and ambassador to Washington, Ardeshir Zahedi, as he hurried to catch a connecting flight at Paris's Charles de Gaulle Airport. The debonair envoy seemed shaken but agreed to be interviewed. It wasn't so much what Zahedi said. That was boilerplate — *the struggle for the soul of Iran will continue*. But he was our only voice from the fallen shah's entourage. It was the day's biggest story.

Peter and I continued our stormy relationship. One Friday night, a massive snowstorm shut down the Bonn–Cologne airport and left me stranded, unable to meet Peter in Paris. In desperation, I persuaded two fellow passengers to share a rental car with me and drive to Paris. I called Peter from an airport phone and told him I was en route — snowstorm be damned! The drive took almost seven hours in terrible conditions. The others, two German businessmen, did the driving. It was midnight when we finally pulled in to Paris. Let's get a bite and a drink, one of them suggested, and celebrate our arrival. They suggested onion soup at the famed Au Pied de Cochon, in Les Halles. I could hardly decline their invitation. They had driven me to Paris.

When I arrived at the Lancaster an hour later, Peter was furious. It did no good for me to explain how dangerous the drive had been, how amazing that I had made it at all. That I had to show my gratitude for the lift by having a bite with the drivers. He was unrelenting in his anger. Knowing he was waiting for me, I should have come straight to the hotel, he said. For the rest of that snowy Paris weekend he barely spoke to me. I flew back to Bonn on Monday bleary-eyed and exhausted.

Things will be better when we live together, I told myself. All these separations are not good for us. We adored each other. Time would calm our fevered passions. "My dearest Katika," he wrote me from Paris, while I was on home leave in New York, "you will not wake up for an hour and the time is crawling by — Time is a centipede today. I am trying to be calm, mindful of your urging, but it isn't easy . . . As I look across the street from the Bureau's fifth floor here and admire the Haussmann balconies I am thinking how much I learn from you and what a great joy it is. I have a hard time thinking back to those days when

I was not particularly fond of Paris. Even without you here, there is so much of *us* in it. (Even if I have to hear for the umpteenth time, 'That's the corner where I lived and there are the paving stones I tore up for the Revolution.') What's difficult about you being in New York is the pressure of the corporation on us as a couple. I have come with a great rush to value privacy more than ever before. That is so true because for the first time privacy — with you — is so profound, so fulfilling. God, can you give up the photographers for that sort of adulation?" In the margin of that letter, Peter had drawn a candle and written beside it: "This is a candle! You are my light."

On February 1, 1979, the ayatollah and his entourage astonished the world. Among the first to learn of Khomeini's sudden return trip to Iran was Peter. "Darling," he wrote me, "have returned from lunch to find that Khomeini is leaving tonight . . . and I'm going with him! Pray for me — It sounds bad and I have to convince myself that what is bad is my imagination in situations like this. I love you, will love you always, through thick and thin and thick — there has been no thin for us. I miss you with a pain in my heart — I want you. I want and need us."

Khomeini boarded a Tehran-bound Air France 747 in Paris, accompanied by Peter and 140 other journalists. The plane did not have permission to land in Iran. It was a very dangerous mission, but Peter would never turn down such an assignment. En route, he scored an exclusive interview with the ayatollah. "How do you feel about being back in Iran?" Peter asked him. "I feel nothing," the imam answered. I was not surprised. Based on my own observations, I judged Khomeini to be emotionally dead.

Tumultuous crowds welcomed the cleric's return. Ghotbzadeh and his other faithful servants had done a masterly job preparing the way. In March, 98 percent of the population voted in favor of replacing the shah's regime with an Islamic republic. Khomeini himself became Supreme Leader in November. Three years later our friend, the forty-six-year-old, handsome Sadegh, Khomeini's "almost son," was led before a firing squad and executed. In the harsh theocracy of the mullahs, there was no room for westernized secular figures such as Sadegh Ghotbzadeh. The Islamic revolution was consuming its own. I think of him each time I am at the Closerie des Lilas. "Look at his face," Sadegh once said to me, indicating Khomeini. "He can only be a good man."

Peter and I continued our roller-coaster ride of passionate reunions and agonizing separations through the next year. In the spring, the network again tried to lure Peter back to New York. I wrote to Peter from London, "I am sitting just where you and I sat at Brown's Hotel — having tea. This is the first moment I've had since our dramatic night of phone calls. Roone's summons is not what stands out in my mind. Your question, 'Will you come?' does. It was so important for me to hear that. And to hear my reaction — which came without the slightest hesitation from the deepest part of me. It almost doesn't matter what happens now. I want you to be happy — and right now I think New York has an almost symbolic importance for you.* So I hope you and Mr. Wizard [Roone Arledge] can come to terms. You and I have, I think. I feel good and strong and calm about us. I do not feel I have to give up a part of myself for you.

*Peter had been ABC News anchor once before, in the sixties, before he was ready for it. It was then that he began his apprenticeship as a serious television journalist, covering the civil rights movement and the Vietnam War, before becoming the network's chief foreign correspondent, based in London.

That wouldn't make either of us happy. I feel I am growing, stretching beside you. I somehow feel a much fuller person with you than I ever have without you. Which does not preclude a strong professional side. I think we can work that out together." Reading this now, I sound as if I am trying mightily to persuade myself of this less than obvious fact.

Later that year, Peter flew from our London home to Tehran to cover the militants' seizure of American diplomats and others as hostages. President Jimmy Carter had bowed to intense pressure from friends of the shah — notably Henry Kissinger — and admitted the exiled monarch to the United States. The ayatollah's followers retaliated by seizing the American Embassy in Tehran and taking fifty-three hostages. *America Held Hostage* was more than the name of a new nightly ABC News broadcast anchored by Ted Koppel. It expressed the shock and humiliation of a nation, and eventually drove a president from the White House. Almost the minute Jimmy Carter's limousine rolled out of the White House, Tehran released the American hostages — yet another jab at the country that Khomeini's supporters had dubbed the Great Satan.

Microphone in hand, I stood on the frozen tarmac of Frankfurt Airport when the freed hostages landed, and interviewed them for NPR radio. They looked much thinner but as wan as the defeated American president.

I had given up my post as ABC News bureau chief in Germany. Carrying on a long-distance love affair with Peter while reporting for ABC News proved too stressful. I moved to London during the summer of 1979, already pregnant with Elizabeth. Peter continued to resist the network's attempts to lure him back to New York and became *World News Tonight*'s overseas anchor. We married in early September and moved into a charming but derelict rowhouse in Notting Hill. I threw myself into its renovation and into my new domestic role with the same zeal with which I once attacked unmasking corruption in Philadelphia and spy stories in Germany. It was clear to me that I could not combine life as Peter's wife, the mother of his child, with the life of a full-time foreign correspondent.

With Peter by my side for eleven hours of natural childbirth, Elizabeth Ilona Marton Jennings arrived on September 29, 1979. It was the happiest day of my life. Peter returned to Tehran a few weeks later and stayed away for six weeks. By the time he returned, Lizzie was sleeping through the night and our house renovation was complete. When Christopher Charles Jennings was born two and a half years later, we moved to a bigger house, with a bigger garden, in Hampstead. This pile needed even more extensive renovation than our Notting Hill rowhouse.

Maternal and marital bliss did not snuff out my other dreams and ambitions, however. While still nursing Lizzie, I wrote a lengthy essay about the Polish pope, John Paul II. It was a long shot, but I sent it off to the *Atlantic*. I still have the telegram I received from the magazine's editor. "Vatican piece excellent. Letter follows." Titled "The Paradoxical Pope," my story made the magazine's May 1980 cover. It was an unaccustomed thrill to see that cover on newsstands, with my byline under the pope's portrait. Television, an ephemeral medium, did not give me that same sense of satisfaction.

The next article I wrote for the *Atlantic* was also made a cover. It was a profile of a then obscure Swedish diplomat who had saved thousands of Jews in Budapest during the last months of World War II, only to be taken prisoner by the Red Army. His name was Raoul Wallenberg, and that story changed my life. It became my first book.

In the process of researching the biography of the Swedish hero, I learned of my Jewish roots. While interviewing a woman in Budapest who had been rescued by Wallenberg, she remarked matter-of-factly, "Unfortunately, Wallenberg arrived too late for your maternal grandparents." We were Jewish. Raised Roman Catholic, I was shocked to learn this. I had been told my grandparents died under an Allied bombing raid. So many Hungarians had — I had no reason to question this.

I called my parents that evening from Budapest. "Why didn't you tell me?" I asked my father. He turned cold and did not want to discuss our roots, or how my parents survived while my grandparents did not. "You will never understand any of this," he said flatly. "You are an American. You have no idea what we went through. We were never Jewish. We were not religious people. We were Hungarians."

I returned to Budapest a number of times, each time learning a little more about our family history. My great-grandfather, I discovered from Jewish archives, Maurice Mandl, born in 1848, was the son of the chief rabbi of Dobris, Bohemia. German was his mother tongue, Franz Joseph his emperor. In his early twenties, he jumped onto a rickety train to Budapest. He soon learned Hungarian and rode the crest of Budapest's golden years in the late nineteenth century. His rabbi father traveled from Bohemia to Budapest only once, to officiate at Maurice's wedding in the Great Synagogue on Dohany Street in 1876. Somewhere along the way they *magyarized* their name from Mandl to Marton. Maurice and his wife, Tekla, had six children, among them, in the style of the newly emancipated and secular Hungarian Jews, a lawyer, an engineer, a teacher, and a grain merchant, my grandfather. Great-grandfather Maurice's apartment in Budapest's fashionable Leopoldtown overlooked the Danube. His sons were decorated in World War I. Thirty years later, his grandsons were forbidden to wear their country's uniform or to bear arms. They — my father among them — were sent off to forced labor on the Russian Front.

The Martons stayed through the Nazi terror, which they barely survived. My maternal grandparents were less fortunate. Living in the northeast city of Miskolc, they were among the first Jews rounded up by Adolf Eichmann and his Hungarian allies and forced onto an Auschwitz transport. The last word my mother had from her parents was a postcard slipped through the crack of a cattle car headed for the death camp.

With my insistent explorations of our family history, for the first time in his new life in America my father had lost control of his own narrative. My parents, bruised survivors of the twentieth century, were not pleased with my probing. For quite a while, our bond frayed, and they kept their distance. Peter was wonderful during this painful time for me. "How much more interesting to have a Jewish wife," he said, "than a lapsed Catholic." He played mediator between my parents and me, and slowly we healed the rift. Peter returned from one of his Middle East trips with a beautiful ring he had made for me from an early Jewish coin minted in the Holy Land. I still treasure it.

Wallenberg changed my life in another way. I decided to become a full-time writer. It was a big leap: from knocking out minute-and-a-half television scripts to writing a full-size book. Peter could not have been more supportive. To encourage me, he had the ABC art department make up a framed sign that said, "One page at a time, One day at a time. You are a great talent." He hung it on the wall over my desk, where it stayed.

When I finished *Wallenberg*, I remember Peter's mother, a woman I admired for her elegance and dry wit, saying, "Well, Kati, I hope you got *that* out of your system." She meant writing books. But I had not. I was already at work on the second.

I had a moment of clarity. The children and I were staying at my mother-in-law's house in Ottawa. Lizzie and Chris, perfect English tots, had composed a poem to their granny. I did not want to be in the room when they recited it, as I knew I would be reduced to tears. So, from around the corner, I listened to them stumbling over their childish ode. From Granny Jennings only silence. Poking my head around the corner, I asked, Did you like it, Granny? "Yes, dear," she answered, crisply. "But no sense giving them a big head with too much praise." Oh, I said to myself. That is how you raised your son, too. And no amount of love on my part will ever fill that deficit.

But we were so happy as a family, doting on our beautiful children and our new house in Hampstead. Peter could still be the world's most loving, irresistible charmer. When the *Atlantic* published my story about the missing Swede, Peter wrote me a "fan letter." "I just wanted to say that I read your article on that Swedish fellow in the *Pacific Monthly* and the way you put things together, I just wanted to say, aw shucks, it would be worth going missing to have you start out in search of me. Signed, a Fan."

Bleary-eyed from night feeds, I struggled to hang on to my precarious identity as a writer. *Wallenberg*'s strong reception gave me a huge boost, however. The *Washington Post* reviewer wrote that my work "excels in descriptions of her native Hungary and the Soviet Gulag . . . and the sensitive treatment of personalities involved. It is the best written of the four [Wallenberg biographies] and may well become the standard Wallenberg biography." I was encouraged by letters from all over the world. The distinguished French film director Louis Malle wrote, "I just finished reading *Wallenberg* and was deeply moved by the tragedy of his life . . . which seems to come right out of Kafka . . . Your book is wonderfully written and I was very impressed by the care and thoroughness you put into researching this incredibly complex life story."

I also started writing a column for the London *Times*, mostly on the theme of British sexism — something I was experiencing as a pregnant (again), no-longer-employed "mum." "It was during my first London dinner party," I wrote in my October 30, 1982, column, "that I was initiated into my new status as woman-to-be-seen-not-heard."

But not even my more housebound life as a freelance writer and full-time mother calmed our explosive relationship. "I wish sometimes that I didn't have these weird bouts of *need*," Peter wrote to me from a reporting trip to Budapest. "But I never wish I didn't love you as much as I do (even when it hurts). I do not wish ever to be with *anyone else*."

The very qualities that my family and friends encouraged — my irreverence and my drive — through Peter's eyes became liabilities. "Glib," he called me, and "ambitious." I vowed to change — to transform myself into a London "mum," content to push Lizzie and Chris's prams in Holland Park and Hampstead Heath. What could be so hard about that?

We eventually accepted the network's call to move to New York. Here is how Peter described our decision: "My first instinct was to say no, altogether. Kati was the one who convinced me this was a very important job and you didn't just say no idly. We had

145

a long, very difficult time in deciding to come."

Things changed irrevocably for us once we moved to New York. The relentless public attention and pressure to stay at the very top of the network's precarious summit slowly eroded our intimacy. My husband became a star — America's favorite anchor. We lived what seemed a dream life: a golden couple in Gotham. To a large degree, the week's news ratings governed his mood, and there was always another one coming.

On June 16, 1989, Peter and I stood side by side in a sea of 300,000 Hungarians in Budapest's Heroes' Square and shared a powerful and, for me, personal moment. The reburial of the fallen leaders of the 1956 uprising marked the ceremonial end of Communist rule. Though my parents and I were not together for this deeply satisfying moment, we had lived to see the fall of the twentieth century's second destructive movement. My joy was reflected in the tear-stained faces on that crowded Budapest square.

Despite his great talent and tremendous success, Peter was an insecure man. He never got over the stigma he felt regarding his lack of a formal education. Combined with an emotionally chilly mother, this bred his insecurities but also fueled his drive to reach the very top of his profession. Peter was both proud of my multilingual education and resentful of my two college degrees. He also thought I was overly confident, and needed taking down a peg. He enjoyed throwing me off balance. But he was as hard on himself as he was on me.

Once, en route to a Washington dinner in honor of Prince Charles and Princess Diana, Peter, appraising my black velvet strapless gown, asked, "Are you sure you want to wear *that?*" Seated next to Prince Charles, I spent the evening tugging self-consciously at my décolletage, anxious not to offend His Royal Highness with the display. The other thing I recall about that dinner was that every time the prince moved his chin five inches to the left, a courtier on bended knee would appear.

Ten years into our marriage, I fell in love with a warm, funny, loving man who did not think me glib or overly ambitious, just funny. I told Peter I had found happiness and did not think I could give it up. He pleaded and I stayed. I could not bear breaking up our family. During the next six years, Peter and I raised our children and I wrote two more books.* But I missed the bone-deep happiness we once had, without which I could not thrive. I began to think that Peter loved the *idea* of me. In reality, he was searching for a wife who would fill the role his mother had not: a full-time supporter of all his efforts and needs, only minimally distracted by her own.

*The Polk Conspiracy — Murder and Cover-up in the Case of CBS Correspondent George Polk (New York: Farrar, Straus & Giroux, 1990) and *A Death in Jerusalem* (New York: Pantheon, 1994).

I arrived in Paris in the Spring of 1978 as ABC News foreign correspondent, just a decade after my abrupt departure from the city in May 1968, when it was caught up in violent demonstrations.

Peter in London shortly after our wedding in September 1979.

In front of St. Peter's in Rome. Peter and I covered the induction of Pope John Paul II in October 1978.

Early in our courtship, I took Peter to my hometown, Budapest, one of the few cities in the world he had never visited. He loved it.

This shot of Peter and me was taken by Richard Avedon when he photographed Peter for a *GQ* magazine cover in 1985.

Our new family—Peter, Lizzie and me, the proud new mother, in front of our Notting Hill Gate house in London, 1981.

With Christopher and Lizzie in the garden of our London house in 1982.

Peter and I covered several Communist Party Congresses in Moscow in the seventies and eighties.

Peter and I took our two-week-old son to Ascot in June 1982.

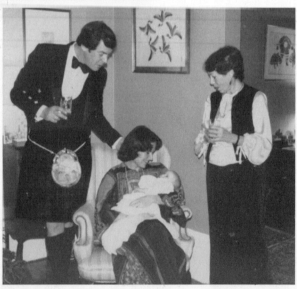

Elizabeth Marton Jennings' first Christmas—in London, with my mother and Peter in the Scottish kilt he always wore at Christmas.

In 2000, Richard and I revisited Chartres where we had spent our first day together, at Christmas 1993. We are standing in front of La Vieille Maison, the restaurant where we had our first meal in France.

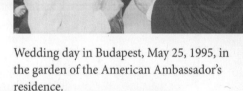

Wedding day in Budapest, May 25, 1995, in the garden of the American Ambassador's residence.

David and Anthony Holbrooke at their father's Budapest wedding in May 1995.

A dinner we hosted for President Bill Clinton at our Waldorf residence when Richard was United Nations Ambassador in 1999. My husband always insisted that I give the welcoming toast at these events. Here I am raising my glass to the president, while Harrison Ford, Caroline Kennedy, and Elizabeth Rohatyn look on.

With Kofi Annan, the UN Secretary General and our dear friend whom I had known since the eighties. I met him during my research on Raoul Wallenberg, who was the uncle of Annan's wife, Nane.

Sharing a laugh with Nelson Mandela at his home in Johannesburg, South Africa. It was a privilege to have him as our houseguest several times when Richard was UN Ambassador.

Visiting Kabul, Afghanistan, in 2006. The land and its troubles made a deep impression on Richard and me. This trip—arranged by my nephew Mathieu Marton Lefevre, a UN political officer in Kabul—was the beginning of my husband's deep involvement with the region.

While on an AIDS mission to Botswana, Richard and I explored the spectacular Okavango.

The legendary photographer Henri Cartier-Bresson, whom I interviewed on the subject of his partner at Magnum Photo, Robert Capa, in his Paris apartment overlooking the Tuileries Garden, 2004.

In Telluride, Colorado, with our close friends, Samantha Power and Cass Sunstein, in 2008. Samantha was Richard's protégé and my steadfast companion during Richard's final days and the months that followed.

Richard and I look ecstatic following a zip-lining adventure in the Costa Rican rain forest during Christmas 2005.

With General Roméo Dallaire and two former child soldiers while I worked on this issue at the UN in 2002.

At Samantha and Cass's wedding in 2008 in Ireland.

My daughter, Lizzie, and I on the Pont des Arts in Paris in 2006.

Richard and I were guests of the Norwegian Red Cross on a hiking trip in 2003.

I am standing between President Obama and President Clinton and
Secretary of State Hillary Clinton, looking out at the audience of mourners
during the Kennedy Center memorial for Richard in January 2011. I wear a
very forced smile.

Hillary Clinton proved a staunch friend to both Richard and me before, during, and after Richard's illness and death. Here we are at the Asia Society in New York in February 2001. The Secretary of State has just delivered a major policy speech about Afghanistan and Pakistan which she dedicated to Richard. Jordan's Queen Noor is standing to the left.

With my son, Chris, in Paris in 2000. I am thrilled that both Chris and Lizzie love the city almost as much as I do.

Chris and Lizzie in my Paris apartment, Christmas 2011.

My sister, Juli, with the latest member of the Marton family, her son Mathieu's first born, Lucien.

Christmas 2011 in the Luxembourg Gardens—the start of our new family tradition of spending the holidays in Paris.

The start of a new life, alone, in Paris.

■ ■ ■ ■

PART IV

■ ■ ■ ■

We always returned to [Paris] no matter
who we were or how it was changed
or with what difficulties, or ease, it
could be reached. Paris was always
worth it and you received return for
whatever you brought to it.
— Ernest Hemingway, *A Moveable Feast*

Chapter Eleven

It is Christmas 1993. I am spending the holidays at my sister's house just outside Paris, with Elizabeth, now fourteen, and Chris, twelve. After fifteen turbulent years, I have left Peter. It was a seemingly trivial incident that finally decided it. A few months earlier, in late summer 1993, we were just leaving a party in East Hampton at the home of our friends Howard and Jennifer Stringer. Standing in their driveway as others were saying good night, I turned to my husband and said, "Shall we go, sweetheart?" In answer, Peter tossed the car keys at me and said, "You can go, if you want." I felt humiliated in front of our friends and vowed never again to submit to such looks of pity and embarrassment.

The next morning, when Peter and the children packed the car to begin our annual family vacation in Canada, I told Peter I would join them later. Later that day, I called him in Ottawa and told him I wanted a divorce. It was a cowardly way to break the news, but I knew he would try to stop me from leaving, as he had done before, if I asked him in person.

By Christmas, Peter had not yet moved out of our apartment. He was sleeping on a couch, and life was unbearably tense.

In Paris, my sister, Juli, is her steady self and we are determined to produce our usual festive Christmas for our children, her two and my two. Paris never looks more magical than at Christmas, when the shops dazzle with tiny white lights, and the food markets show off their delicately arranged, rosy filets of beef, pearly fish in heaps, and, of course, the dizzying array of cheeses, fruits, and pastries. With our four children in tow, we shop for our feast of roast goose and chestnuts. I marvel at the pride with which the butcher presents us our goose, and how lovingly he slips paper socks on the bird's legs. I am feigning a festive spirit I do not feel. I feel lost.

I have passed forty and I have no sense of my own future. I am exhausted from trying to keep our family together, from the high-wire act of our marriage, often played out in the media. It was assumed I was leaving because I could not adjust to life in the giant shadow of Peter's celebrity. Our problems went so much deeper than tabloid reports, of course. But so did the ties that bound us. Their names were Elizabeth and Christopher.

On Christmas Day, Peter arrived at my sister's house. He said he wanted to try one last time to save our marriage. "Our family," he said. I wasn't leaving him, but "our family." I adored our children. I wanted more than anything to preserve *us*. I was still torn, still conflicted, I still loved him, but I could not stay with him. Time and breathtaking professional success did not diminish his bouts of jealousy and insecurity. Moreover, I had given him cause for his anger: I had confessed to an affair and then stayed when he pleaded with me to try one more time to save our marriage.

After Peter's arrival, I did not want to stay in my sister's house. So, on Christmas Day Peter drove me to a nearby hotel. He said he was giving me until spring to "figure things out."

It was my choice, but I felt very alone — a particularly bitter feeling at Christmas. But I did not need until spring to figure things out.

A friend — not close, but someone whose

company I had enjoyed over the years — had called the day before, reaching me at my sister's house. He said he heard I was in Paris, heard about my situation. "Really sorry, and hope it's for the best," he said. He had just driven over from Germany, he said, and was staying at the residence of the American ambassador, Pamela Harriman. "Christmas is no time to be alone," he said. "How about a little trip to cheer you up? What's your favorite spot in France?" Before I could even pause to think, I blurted out "the Loire valley." I remembered happy days there as a student.

On December 26, an armored Buick the size of a small tank, the official car of the American ambassador to Germany, rolled up the gravel drive of the Hotel Petit Trianon in Versailles. Ambassador Richard Holbrooke was behind the wheel. I stood on that gravel path, my frozen hands jammed in the pockets of my camelhair coat, and wondered what the hell I was doing. Taking in my swollen, red-rimmed eyes, Richard, radiating excitement and good cheer, said, "C'mon! Let's go!" I jumped in. Our lives are turned in such split seconds.

The weather was gray and bone chilling

and matched my mood perfectly. As we meandered toward the Loire valley, my mind was far from Richard or our little trip. I was wondering what my kids — with their father and my sister in Paris — were doing just then, and were they missing their mother at Christmas? Watching the wintry landscape roll by, I hoped Richard did not notice the tears that kept flowing. Had I just made the biggest mistake of my life? I saw no future, just the mistakes of the past. Frequently blowing my nose, I warned Richard I would be terrible company. He did not seem to mind.

We stopped in Chartres. We found just the right restaurant near the cathedral, an old-fashioned country inn called La Vieille Maison. A fire roared in the gabled dining room and the maître d' seated us next to it. Richard knew his way around French menus and ordered for us both. The food was wonderful and the wine warm against the winter chill. I was relieved to be with someone who expected nothing more than my presence. He was burrowed in a book about the great cathedral from which he was reading out loud to me. Suddenly, he looked up and saw someone he recognized passing in front of the restaurant's plate glass window. Jumping up, Richard walked right into the glass front door. I could not suppress a smile at this scene from a *Road Runner* cartoon.

Rubbing his forehead, he returned to the table. "That guy is the greatest living guide to Chartres and I wanted him to give you a tour," he explained. "I missed him." I was charmed by this man who had driven so far to have lunch with a woman in such a miserable state, only to be rewarded with an angry bump on his forehead. This was not the Richard Holbrooke I knew, mostly from the Council on Foreign Relations and television interviews.

It was twilight when we left the restaurant, the gray sky blending into the ancient stones. Smoke rising from chimneys gave the town a timeless feeling. Inside the cathedral, the famous blue in the stained-glass windows shone brightly even in the dim light. We sat in a pew, enveloped by the smell of incense and the hush of a winter evening. But even in this stillness, Richard was irrepressible. "Just imagine," he whispered urgently, "the pilgrims' first reaction to the sight of these windows! The power of this place for medieval peasants."

For five days we visited Loire châteaux. Richard kept up a steady stream of stories of royal intrigue and dynastic blood-spilling. His excitement on the subject of French architecture and history was contagious. He preferred the more earthbound Romanesque to the soaring Gothic that it begat. The winter days were short and each night we stayed in places he had circled in his *Guide Michelin*. He knew so much French history, and read passages from old guidebooks he had since 1968, which he had brought along from Germany.

In Tours, I was the guide. I showed him the *maison particulière* on the rue Jules Simon, where I had stayed with the family of Count Clouet. The garden of the Cathédrale St.-Gatien, where I once sat by flower beds the color of the setting sun, was now covered with frost. He laughed when I described my earnest, enchanted, Francophile self of two decades earlier. "You are so different in France than in New York!" he exclaimed. You, too, I thought.

We drove back to Paris and he asked me where we should spend our last night before he returned to Berlin and I to New York. Place des Vosges, I said impulsively. So he booked us two rooms at the Pavillon de la Reine. Tucked deep inside one of the arcades, the hotel is almost invisible from the square. Our gabled rooms had low ceilings and a rustic feel, and the hotel seemed a world away from the lights and the bustle of

Paris. I called my children, who told me they were having fun skiing in the Alps with their father, my sister, and their cousins. My heart constricted for just a moment. But I knew I was where I was, by choice.

"I know just the place for our last dinner!" Richard said. "Chez Benoit. Haven't been there in years," he said, "but it's an authentic Parisian bistro. We won't run into anyone we know."

He was right about the authentic part, but otherwise dead wrong. The first person we spotted as we entered Benoit's cozy warmth was Ambassador Pamela Harriman, dining with two New York society figures. I headed for the ladies' room and told Richard to explain to his old friend the need for discretion, as Peter and I were still married. I needn't have worried. Though Pam had been a guest in my home, and I in hers, she had never before seen me without Peter. Now she had no idea who I was. She was focused entirely on Richard.

The next day, Pam put out the word that Holbrooke was seen dining in Paris with a mysterious Swedish journalist. Not worth the trouble learning her name, she told a mutual friend of ours. "Dick" goes through so many women. That was fine with me. In years to come, Richard loved to tell this story as a perfect illustration of Pam Harriman's absolute indifference to women not in a position to do anything for her.

Pam was an important figure in Richard's life. Her husband, the man Richard always called the Governor — W. Averell Harriman — picked Richard, a callow twenty-five-year-old Foreign Service officer, as the youngest member of the Vietnam peace talks in 1968. His title was "Expert," only he didn't know what he was supposed to be expert in.

He thought Pam was doing a superb job as ambassador. When once I asked him why she was so effective in representing her country at the Élysée Palace, he answered, "Four words: Pamela *Digby Churchill Harriman*. The French love all that history."

Somehow, Pam's unexpected presence, and the reminder that we were about to part and return to our very different lives — he to Germany and I to New York — after five surprisingly stress-free days, shifted our mood.

We had talked about every subject: politics, history, art, our shared love of French culture — everything except us. During that final dinner in Paris, we began to cross from banter into different territory.

Richard told me he had been anticipating

my separation for years. He proceeded to list about a decade of sightings of me at parties, meetings, and even in elevators. I was astonished. He had never given away his more than friendly interest in me, even when the two of us would have lunch alone once a year or so. Now I was bemused at how openly he talked about his feelings. He said he had known for years I was just right for him, intellectually and emotionally, and in other ways, too. I had never known a man so comfortable with his own feelings — nor so confident. I did not yet know that this was the same patience, perseverance, and focus Richard brought to the negotiating table — applied to his personal life.

We walked back to the place des Vosges, warmed by the food and wine against the biting cold of the Parisian night. He put his arm around me and I felt very secure there. We circled the place before going into the Pavillon. He took my hand for the first time. That, too, felt natural. We discovered great hand-holding compatibility: not too tight, not too loose. For the next seventeen years, even when watching TV, we held hands.

When he drove me to Charles de Gaulle Airport next day, I felt more hopeful about the future than when I had arrived two weeks earlier.

Hours later, when I walked into my New York apartment, the phone was ringing. I remember thinking, I hope it's Richard. And it was.

CHAPTER TWELVE

Our love story unfolded over the telephone. There has never been a better talker than Richard Holbrooke. The surprise was that he was a good listener, too.

He installed a special phone line in his Bonn residence, and soon in Berlin as well (so the American taxpayer would not be subsidizing our nightly phone sessions, he said). Sometimes we talked for two hours. They were the easiest conversations of my life. He was interested in everything: my children, my writing, my parents, and soon, my painful divorce. His observations about the world were original and based mostly on his own experiences. I don't remember ever hearing him utter a single cliché. Nor did he let me get away with much. "Be precise!" he would say in an attempt to tame my Hungarian love of a good yarn. "Facts are sacred."

He laughed when I used what he called a

"ten-dollar word" to impress him. "Jejune!" he'd tease. "Where did you learn that word, refugee girl?" I confessed to keeping a list of new words as I was still self-conscious about my English. Now I had someone to whom I could show off.

I began to follow the news differently. Through Richard, I felt that I was inside the room where events unfolded — and not only in the present. The players took on real personalities. I was no longer a journalist, my nose pressed against the window of big events. I soon felt that I knew Bill Clinton, Jimmy Carter, Lyndon Johnson, General William Westmoreland, Bobby Kennedy, and even FDR and Woodrow Wilson — personally. It was exhilarating. But he was just as passionate about lower forms of art. We would "watch" David Letterman's show together, he in Germany, through a special feed, me in New York. "You *cannot* go to sleep until we hear Letterman's top-ten list," he would insist, as I was dropping off.

It was the purest courtship of my life. We had only the sound of each other's voices on the telephone. In a month's time, we were deeply enmeshed in each other's lives, thoughts, dreams, and ambitions. In those pre-email days, we faxed back and forth, sending things we were writing, for the other's comments. It is hard for me to imagine getting through that period of hurt and disappointment, ending fifteen years of marriage, without Richard's mellow "Hel-lo Katika" at the day's end. He was calm and unflappable in family crises — mediating my conflicts with my children and parents. He was more easily moved by historic events than by human foibles. Years later, when he met with the newly elected president, Barack Obama, in Chicago, he teared up at the enormity of the moment: shaking hands with our country's first African-American president. Richard did not think his show of emotion went down well with Mr. Obama.

In 1994, I was relieved that Richard was far away. Lizzie and Chris adored both their parents and were pained to see our family come apart. I was desperately trying to be loving and present for them, while dealing with Peter's anger. For a very long time Peter refused to move out of our apartment. Whatever his role in our marriage, I was the initiator of our divorce. Our children covering their parents' bed with rose petals, and lighting candles in our bedroom — one of Chris and Lizzie's final attempts to bring us back together — is still a searing memory.

Richard visited me in late January, and I

spent some days with him in both Bonn and Berlin in February. The absence of drama in our relationship was an adjustment for me. I had never before been in love with a man who was so *un*elusive. He said he had waited a long time for me, and I was for him, and that was that. He had been single for two decades and did not want to waste any time. When we disagreed, he would cut the argument short. "Look," he would say, "you and I both know where we want this to come out, so let's just get there fast."

After so many years expending emotional energy on my volatile marriage, I suddenly had energy to spare. I finished my fourth book, *A Death in Jerusalem*, on the assassination of the first Arab-Israeli peace negotiator, Count Folke Bernadotte; became chair of the Committee to Protect Journalists; and soon started a new book.

One night as Richard and I were reluctantly winding up a long conversation that neither of us wanted to end, I said teasingly, "Well, maybe when you come home, in a couple of years, we should try living together." Oh no, he answered. "I'm too old for that. I did that with Diane Sawyer for seven years." "Okay then," I teased. "I guess we just have to get married."

The next morning my fax machine disgorged the following note, on the letterhead of the United States ambassador to Germany: "Ambassador Richard C. Holbrooke accepts with great pleasure the offer of marriage to Miss Kati Marton, at a date to be determined." A few days later the mail brought an elegant, gold embossed card, complete with the ambassadorial seal, with the following handwritten poem, dated April 14, 1994:

Wilt Thou be mine — As I am Thine,
With or without this rhyme?

The card sits today in a silver frame on my dresser.

Later that winter of 1994, he joined me in Budapest, where I was working on a travel piece. Walking down the Andrassy Boulevard, hand in hand, I felt that I was home, really home, for the first time — my past and the present joined. We had a shared attachment to history and were viscerally bound to the violent twentieth century our parents had barely survived. Sitting side by side in Budapest's Great Synagogue, I felt a powerful current pass between us. My great-grandparents had been married in that synagogue by my great-great-grandfather, a rabbi who had traveled from Prague to

166

perform the ceremony. I was just beginning to learn my own history, as my parents had kept all of this hidden. I was outraged by how much they had withheld, but Richard understood them, and was forgiving. "They are survivors," he said, "strong people who lived through things you and I have not. You are here, and you are who you are, because they survived."

In Paris that June, Richard met my family. At lunch at my sister's house, my father, who considered Peter his son-in-law for life, was reserved. My sister, who had drawn very close to Peter, was also aloof. Lizzie ignored him, pretending he wasn't there. Chris had no problem with Richard, but was soon off to boarding school. Richard shrugged all this off as perfectly normal. He liked them, and was sure they would come around. He was absolutely right regarding my daughter and my sister.

Richard continued to admire and engage my father. He considered my parents to be remarkable people, whose like we would not see again. Later, when the opportunity for us to buy the small apartment next door to ours presented itself, Richard said, "Let's buy it for whichever of your parents survives the other." And so we did, and that apartment became my father's final home after my mother's death in September 2004.

During the summer of 1994, Richard and I toured the French countryside, visiting some great restaurants along the way: Guy Savoy, Georges Blanc, and Père Bise were among his favorites. Richard loved the theater of elegant dining, the excitement of the moment when the waiters lift the silver covers in unison, revealing the works of art they contain. He adored the ritual of the pompous waiters, as serious as Shakespearean actors, reciting what we were about to consume, barely looking down at us unworthy Americans.

Sometime during this idyll, Pam Harriman called. She congratulated us on our engagement and said she wanted to host a party in our honor at the Residence. "How sweet!" I said and we quickly accepted. Several days later, we arrived at the splendid mansion on the rue du Faubourg St.-Honoré. Over lunch, our immaculately dressed hostess, with her lofty helmet of bronze hair, said she had some bad news. August, she explained in her plummiest British accent, means the wives of all the "important people" are out of town, vacationing with their children. Sadly, the dinner she planned in our honor would have to be a stag affair, except for her. So unfortunate. But, she smiled at me and said, we'll prepare a lovely tray to send upstairs for you, "Katie" (as she called me). I thought Richard was going to spit out his fish. "Pam" — his blue eyes bored into hers — "that is totally unacceptable!" he spluttered. "Under those circumstances, Kati and I are not going to stay with you." Springing up, barely snatching the napkin out of his collar, he bolted toward the door, with me just behind him.

We checked into the Pavillon de la Reine. If I had not already been in love with him, I would have fallen then. This man knew about loyalty — and priorities.

I also learned something about Pamela Digby Churchill Harriman. The phone was ringing by the time we arrived at our cozy gabled room overlooking the place des Vosges. "Dick," she cooed at him, "I was able to persuade a few wives to return from their vacations for this dinner. I do hope you and Katie will reconsider." We laughed at Pam's ability to turn on a dime when her bluff was called. And we graciously attended the dinner in our honor.

Gradually, Paris became our place. The Left Bank was our side of town — as it had been when I was a student. The Right Bank was business: the embassy on the Avenue Gabriel, the great hotels around the place Vendôme and the Concorde, the Élysée Palace. In the Latin Quarter, we felt like young bohemians. In Paris, Richard slowed down. One night at Le Coupe-Chou, a romantic little place we found just below the Pantheon, he said, "I love your name." "I don't," I replied. "Kati sounds so . . . *trenchant*." "Wow," he said. "That's another ten-dollar word for the refugee." And from then on he called me "T for Trenchant," and pretty soon he was signing his notes to me "T." "We're stronger than dirt," Richard used to say, rather unromantically, I thought. "We won't spend any time with people who don't wish us well." He said that often — and we didn't.

We got married in Budapest, on Memorial Weekend, 1995. It was a beautiful wedding in an emotionally charged place for me: the garden of the American ambassador's residence. In my childhood, my sister and I had spent many afternoons playing hide-and-seek there while our parents were inside talking to the ambassador. Marrying Richard in that garden felt like a circle closed. The president of a new, democratic Hungary, Árpád Göncz, and virtually his whole cabinet were in attendance, as well as my brother, Andrew; Richard's sons; his mother and beloved Uncle Ernie; and some dear friends who had flown in from New York, London, and Berlin. Ambassador and Mrs. Donald Blinken were gracious hosts. I wished that my parents and children had been there. Peter did not encourage their attendance — to say the least — and I decided not to make a big deal out of it. Nothing could really dampen my happiness.

As the freshly minted Mrs. Richard C. Holbrooke, I was about to have an eye-opening experience. Richard and I arrived at the Hotel l'Abbaye de Talloires in Annecy, in the French Alps, for our honeymoon. As my first wifely gesture, I unzipped his suitcase. To my horror, his honeymoon kit contained two suits, one black and one pinstriped, several white shirts, and some funereal ties and a pair of sinister-looking black brogues. "Did you pack for a conference or for your honeymoon?" I asked, Hungarian temper rising. "Gordon must have forgotten where I was going," he answered, blaming his butler at the Berlin Embassy. "Gordon!" I exploded. But before I could vent further about a man who doesn't pack for his own honeymoon, Richard had his jacket on and was pulling me toward the door. "Let's go and buy me clothes *you* want me to wear," he said, smiling, as if this were all part of his plan. "Your taste is so much better than mine — or Gordon's."

Thus did I discover how totally indifferent Richard was to what was on his back. I also discovered the speed with which he could extinguish my temper. Off we drove to the charming Alpine hamlet of Annecy. I can still hear the lady behind the counter of the first boutique we entered. Hearing our tale of a honeymoon emergency, her eyes wide, eyebrows shooting straight up, as if facing two ignorant savages, she blurted out, "Mais, il y a toujours Oxford!" There is always Oxford, the local men's sportswear store — obvious to any fool. After that, when one of us asked a question with an obvious answer, the other would tease, "Mais, il y a toujours Oxford!"

CHAPTER THIRTEEN

The summer of 1995 was the savage season of Srebrenica, when Bosnian Serbs under the brutal General Ratko Mladic butchered thousands of their Muslim countrymen, and humbled the UN peacekeepers charged with protecting them. The Balkan wars had turned too murderous for either Washington or the European powers to avert their gaze any longer. Richard was named peace negotiator and had no time for Parisian weekends.

Six weeks after our wedding, I was jolted from early morning sleep by the State Department Operations Center. "Mrs. Holbrooke," a voice said, "there has been an accident on the road to Sarajevo." I was now sitting bolt upright. "We do not yet have all the details, but several members of your husband's team have suffered serious injuries. Your husband asked us to call you and to tell you he will be calling soon."

As I waited to hear from Richard, I had my first taste of something I was to experience time and again when he traveled to war zones, from the Balkans to Afghanistan and Pakistan. The hard knot of anxiety in the pit of my stomach — waiting for the phone to ring. I never did get used to those trips.

His call came soon enough. "We lost Bob, Joe, and Nelson," Richard said, barely above a whisper, meaning Robert Frasure, Joseph Kruzel, and Nelson Drew, three key members of his negotiating team. "Their APC [armored personnel carrier] rolled down the Igman Road. Ours was behind theirs and we just made it." My husband was alive by a fluke. "I'm bringing their coffins back for burial at Arlington. Please be there," he said.

I had never heard him so deflated. The deaths were caused by the war, specifically by Mladic's refusal to grant Richard's team safe passage, forcing them to take a dangerous, ill-maintained mountain road to Sarajevo.

Secretary of Defense William Perry called next and offered a plane to pick me up at an airstrip near our Long Island home, to fly me to Andrews Air Force Base, outside Washington, in time for Richard's arrival. My husband looked suddenly old, and sagged with fatigue from a night spent on a military plane, his knees jammed against his friends' coffins. I've never been so happy to see anyone in my life.

After the sad Arlington farewells to his comrades, and a meeting with President Clinton and his national security team, Richard turned right around, flying back to the war zone. Exhausted, he seemed more determined than ever to bring the parties to the negotiating table.

The war shadowed every day of our first year together. Richard made trips to visit the kids and me at our beach house in Bridgehampton that summer, bringing the Balkan turbulence with him. On August 27, Lizzie, a gifted rider, was competing in the Hampton Classic Horse Show, and we were hosting a housewarming for our new home. At six o'clock that morning, an NBC crew arrived to set up their equipment for a live interview with Richard on *Meet the Press*. The children and I stumbled sleepily over wires, and watched in dismayed horror as the crew turned our lovely house into a television studio.

Chris and Lizzie and I marveled at how calmly Richard deflected Robert Novak's grilling. "Do you think it's helpful to the negotiations," Novak baited Richard, "to call [Serb leader Radovan] Karadzic a war criminal?" Sitting on our couch wearing shorts, Richard answered, "It's not a question of what I call him or what you call him. There's an international tribunal going on . . . At Srebrenica a month ago, people were taken into a stadium, lined up, and massacred. It was a crime against humanity of the sort that we have rarely seen in Europe, and not since the days of Himmler and Stalin. That's simply a fact and it has to be dealt with. I'm not going to cut a deal that absolves the people responsible for this."

Listening to his measured, brave words, I was willing to put up with any chaos in our personal life. Later that day, Richard left our housewarming party early to catch a military plane back to the Balkans.

Three months later, I was proud to be by his side at the peace conference in Dayton, Ohio, where from time to time he deployed me. On the opening night, he seated me between Slobodan Milosevic and Alija Izetbegovic, the Serbian and Bosnian Muslim leaders, respectively, who just weeks before had been locked in bloody combat. Richard instructed me to make them talk to each other. To break the ice, I told Milosevic that

I had covered Tito's funeral in Belgrade in 1980. "We Hungarians always admired Yugoslavia during the Cold War, for its multiethnic socialism," I said. "What happened to you?" I asked. Milosevic shrugged, as if he were no more than a passive victim of events. As neither Milosevic nor Izetbegovic would even look in the direction of the other, I finally asked in desperation, "How did the war start?" "I did not think it would be so serious," Izetbegovic answered. Milosevic nodded in agreement. "I never thought it would go on so long." I was appalled at this passivity in the face of the destruction they had unleashed. Their callousness made me even prouder of my husband.

Those weeks behind the chain-link fence at Wright-Patterson Air Force Base were among my life's most memorable. To have been present as my husband forged a historic end to Europe's bloodiest war since World War II was a priceless gift. I marveled each night as Richard plotted the next day's negotiating strategy against some of the wiliest and cruelest warlords in the world. There was nothing foreordained about the success of those talks. Quite the contrary — most observers deemed it mission impossible. But Richard was an inspiring negotiator and team leader, generally several moves ahead of his foes. Even his eruptions — calculated to shake Milosevic — were usually preplanned. The talks he led in Dayton not only ended a savage war but laid the foundations for a new, multiethnic Bosnia.

I could see, however, that the Balkan tragedy changed him. "Nothing can be done" was still not in his vocabulary. But to have been as close to the face of evil as he was for the better part of a decade was transformative. A tiny wooden statue of a man with his head bent down and his hands tied behind his back, carved with glass from a piece of wood by a Muslim inmate in a Serb camp, stood on Richard's desk as a reminder. He was an innate optimist who did not believe conflict between "ancient, ethnic tribes" was inevitable. Something, or, more often, *someone*, had to light the fuse. But I observed some of his optimism give way during those years, to an acceptance that there is such a thing as true evil in the world. How otherwise to explain neighbors and former schoolmates turning on each other with murderous rage in the heart of twentieth-century Europe? He hated cynicism, inaction, and defeatism almost as much as evil. Looking back, I see now how much he changed me, and expanded my world in so many ways.

The day after we returned from Dayton, on November 22, 1995, Peter called. "I'd like to do the first interview with Richard if he wins the Nobel Peace Prize," he said. "Can you arrange it?" Of course, I said. I knew that phone call must have been one of his life's toughest. But he was a pro.

CHAPTER FOURTEEN

Following the signing of the Dayton Accords, Richard left the State Department, as he promised me he would, and moved to New York. But two years later he was recalled to public life when President Clinton appointed him ambassador to the United Nations in 1998.

Richard attacked this appointment with all the creativity and gusto with which he embraced every new task.

We approached his new appointment as full partners. We traveled to a dozen African countries together, and were both shocked by the ravages of HIV/AIDS on the continent. During that exhausting trip, I wrote this letter to my family:

December 12, 1999

Dearest Family,
We started in Mali. I did not expect to

feel emotion descending in a plane simply marked "the United States of America" to face the first of many lines of beautifully robed African dignitaries awaiting us. But I was strangely moved. The hotel (named Grand, of course) was very simple and we did not unpack there or anywhere else for thirteen days. The next day I was to address a conference on media, so I worked on my speech while Richard huddled with his staff. The speech went okay given how tired I was. Nadine Gordimer, Peter Arnett and Charlayne Hunter-Gault also spoke. Richard, meanwhile, was with the President (Mali is in the Security Council this term, hence our stop). Then we were off in a long stream of a motorcade, sirens blaring, back to our plane, our real home. En route, I saw Chinese-style murals urging the laconic populace to excel in sports; business; farming. A tough sell in such a poor, easy-going place.

Next stop: Hell. Angola if you prefer. The capital, Luanda, is a city where nothing works inside a collapsed country. The roads are muddy rivers (after a moderate rainfall), garbage mountains nobody notices line the streets — and, the saddest sight of all — gangs of small children roam the city, orphans of the awful war there between two men who hold Angola hostage to their blood feud: Jona Savimbi, the guerilla leader who lost the election but still has an army, vs. Pres. Eduardo Dos Santos. Though they have wrecked their country, neither is willing to call off the feud. I meet with a mesmerizing man: Raphael Marques, recently jailed and tortured for writing about this insane war. He is painfully skinny (lost 20 lbs. in custody) and smiles serenely. I am so moved by his crazy courage I have to turn away. Come with me, I say to him, at the end of our meeting. I want others in our delegation to see him. I decide to risk upsetting protocol and fly across the miserable town to where Richard is meeting the heads of all the U.N. agencies in Angola. Richard is not at all perturbed — he leaves the meeting and talks to my new friend and promised to raise his case (about to go to trial) with President Dos Santos. The American Ambassador, Joe Sullivan, also commits to attending his trial. Raphael is pleased with this sudden high-level attention.

The afternoon is more difficult. We

drive on rutted roads to a refugee camp (Angolans fleeing Savimbi). There are hundreds of people living in tents — so densely packed they must hear their neighbors breathing at night. Yet they've tried to make homes out of them: pots neatly piled in corners, the dirt floor swept — nothing out of place — a strange dignity in despair. Some of the kids have prepared a little show for us. They sing about peace and, with smiles, ask, in song, "Why so many summits, and never any change?"

I am relieved to leave this battered country. We arrive in Namibia on Friday, December 3. It's dark when we land but the air feels clean and the mountains still visible. The roads are smooth and free of garbage. In the morning, we are surrounded by breathtaking scenery — marred by an overwhelming fact. AIDS is killing this paradise — and much of the continent. We have a secret meeting with women who are H.I.V.+; they can't talk about it openly or they'll lose their jobs and families. AIDS is still a huge stigma, which means people aren't getting tested, which means it is spreading unchecked, crushing the so-called African Renaissance.

Dec. 5 — Praetoria, South Africa — small, quite pretty, crime infested (like so much of post-apartheid S.A.). We drive to Nelson Mandela's home in Jo'burg — 1 hour away. He is tall, erect, elegant in a silk print shirt and in total command of himself and the situation. He wears a hearing aid in each ear but is razor sharp. "I have until noon," he tells us at 10 a.m. The time flies. Talk of Angola, the Congo, Burundi (he wants to play mediator wherever possible), the Middle East, East Timor, his respect for Clinton. He says he will never forget George Bush for being the first to call him when he was freed. His new wife Graca Machel is in her own country (Mozambique) on this day, but he lights up at the mention of her. "I'm a pensioner now," he says several times, when we try to tell him what being with him means to us. He clearly likes women and flirts with me! There is no nostalgia or regret in him — rare after giving up power. He knows his moral position is secure and global. We have pictures taken together ("to match the one of you and my daughter," I tell him). I know I am in the presence of the greatest man of our time and for the third time on our trip I am moved to tears.

Monday, Dec. 6 — Harare, Zimbabwe: small, tidy, provincial, familiar. I was here 21 years ago to cover the final days of Ian Smith's racist regime. I feel very old suddenly — the memory of my younger self (pregnant at the time with Lizzie) keeps intruding. It just doesn't seem possible — so many years' passage — when I'm still on a journey of discovery. We stay where I once did: the Meikles, an old British colonial relic where you can easily pretend you are still in Dorset. While Richard meets President Robert Mugabe I meet a recently tortured journalist, Ray Choto. (There is a symmetry to this trip: Richard talks to the torturers, I talk to the tortured.) Like the Angolan, Rafael Marques, Ray is calm and ready to die for his convictions. The big issue here is Zimbabwe's involvement in the seven-country war raging in the Congo, killing Zimbabwe's economy, and many of its youth.

Wednesday, Dec. 8 — Lusaka, Zambia. I hold a rather depressing meeting for journalists. Zambia is poor and AIDS ravaged and averting its gaze from its own crisis. The national denial includes reporters who tell me AIDS is "over-covered" and yet talk about the African potato as a possible cure.

We spend the afternoon in a makeshift shelter (former bus depot) for AIDS orphans. Again, they put on a show for us: they sing and dance with terrific flare — the obvious result of hard work. But the scene is one of despair. Most of them are barefoot, homeless and often prostitute themselves for a living. We give them soccer balls and school supplies — they present me a homemade basket I will always treasure. The weather is so warm and sultry and their faces are so spirited and hopeful and I feel completely awful for them.

Thursday, Dec. 9 — We fly to Kigali, Rwanda. On the way to town our motorcade stops at the genocide memorial. Richard lays a wreath. An elegant tall woman speaks of the million Tutsis killed in the 1994 genocide. Plain wooden crosses fill the hillside. We stay at the Hotel de Milles Collins, scene of some butchery. It feels wrong to enjoy the spectacular view of the "milles collines" or do anything else but remember.

But the local journalists here amaze me. They seem very open, eager to get on with life — not focused on the terrible past. They are such a contrast to the groups I usually meet in the Balkans. I tell them this (in French) and they are pleased. They write down their names in my notebook. Stay in touch, they ask. I hope I do not disappoint them.

Friday, Dec. 10 — Kampala, Uganda. I am really exhausted. I long to stay in one place, to unpack. I look like hell, but address a large gathering of prominent print, radio, TV reporters. They give me an earful about Pres. Museveni's use of colonial sedition laws to jail reporters. I am running out of encouraging words — and steam. Uganda at least is open and honest about its AIDS problem and is slowly turning it around.

Saturday, Dec 11 — We land in the Heart of Darkness. The real point of this exhausting odyssey: the Congo. Kinshasa bristles with security, uniforms, weapons. We catch a few remnants of the long Belgian rule in the villas we pass in our high-speed motorcade. We are led by a truckload of soldiers brandishing AK-47s. We follow the ritual: Richard and his team go off to the Palace to meet with Pres. Kabila. I meet with a large group of unhappy reporters. They can't report on much while their country is at war. Their wages are pathetic — which leaves them open to officials' bribes. I keep looking out over their heads at the meandering Congo River. How many horrors it has witnessed: the local slave traders, the Belgians, Mobutu, now Kabila. The richer the country — and the Congo is one of the richest — the tougher the road. Can we take off? Our motorcade tears through Kinshasa. Wheels up! Richard and I have bought champagne and smoked salmon for the weary team. Ties are loosed and shoes kicked off for the first time. We land in Niger at midnight to refuel. Another welcoming ceremony. Another beautifully robed president. We are too tired to admire.

I love you all.

K. / Mom

P.S. As Voltaire once said (to whom?), "I apologize, but I did not have time to write a shorter letter."

Following this eye-opening journey, Richard vowed to put AIDS on the UN Security Council's agenda, which he managed to do despite resistance from even the secretary-general, our friend Kofi Annan. It was the first time a health issue has ever been thus treated. The Security Council (the body made up of five permanent members — the United States, Russia, China, France, and the United Kingdom — as well as ten short-term, rotating members) executes UN decisions and normally deals only with issues deemed to be urgent for international security. Richard persuaded the council that the spread of AIDS left unchecked was such an issue. It was a remarkable feat and dramatically altered the way the disease has been treated ever since.

He also brought the UN's most notorious critic, right-wing North Carolina senator Jesse Helms, into the Security Council, and converted him from foe to friend. This was all part of Richard's quest to get the United States to pay over $900 million in back dues to the world body. We knew he had succeeded when Senator Helms wore a blue UN baseball cap to the party we hosted for him.

It was an exhilarating time for us. For the first time in my life, everything seemed aligned and balanced — the personal and the professional, the external and the internal, harmonizing as never before. We felt like two kids suddenly granted their fondest wishes in a fairy tale, as we assembled an art collection that included Jasper Johns,

Willem de Kooning, Richard Tuttle, Maya Lin, several Rauschenbergs, and a Winslow Homer, from American collections made available for the UN ambassador's residence. In waging dinner table diplomacy, we made maximum use of our new official home. We entertained constantly, and always with a purpose.

As our first houseguests, we invited two former residents of the Waldorf apartment, George and Barbara Bush, who lived there from 1971 to 1973, when the elder Bush was Richard Nixon's envoy to the world body. President Bush hugged our housekeeper, Dorothy, who had served his family as well. Taking the tall, former president by the hand, the short, West Indian Dorothy led him to the room where his mother, Dorothy Walker Bush, used to stay. Richard and I stood back as President Bush peered into the small guest room and emerged with eyes moist from memories.

It was the night before the 1999 New Hampshire primary, when his son, George W. Bush, was seeking the Republican nomination for the presidency. "Are you prepared for your son to lose?" I teased President Bush over dinner. His answer astonished me. Without missing a beat, he said, "You know, Jeb would make a fine presidential candidate." It was a revealing statement about Bush family dynamics, which I recalled often during the next eight years of George W. Bush's White House tenure. (George W. Bush did, in fact, lose the New Hampshire primary to John McCain.)

In a letter dated February 1, 2000, President Bush wrote:

Dear Dick and Kati,

As far as Barbara and I go, you hit a home run with bases loaded last night. First we got to stay where once we lived. Many happy memories came rushing back.

Then there was that unique format which made the dinner so different and interesting . . . who says Al Gore invented connectivity? You guys did!

So the bottom line is thanks a million for reaching out across the dreadful party lines and welcoming us into your home, giving us the key to the bedroom in the process.

Sincerely,
George Bush

P.S. I meant what I said about what you've been doing at the UN Security Council.

Before official dinners, Richard and I would sprawl on our bed with seating plans, moving names around a large board like a pair of generals planning a battle, even as the first guests were arriving. For Richard, seating was the key to a great party. We liked unexpected combinations: Whoopi Goldberg next to George Soros, for example. We mixed movie stars such as Robert De Niro, Sarah Jessica Parker, and Charlize Theron with UN ambassadors, senators, and congressmen from both sides of the aisle, transformed suddenly into starstruck fans.

Richard always insisted that I give the welcoming toast, which he maintained I did better than he. I approached this task with some seriousness, and tried to be both witty and topical. Barbara Walters, who had reduced me to tears in Germany many years before, when I was a young foreign correspondent, was a regular at our parties. After a dinner honoring First Lady Hillary Rodham Clinton, Barbara wrote, "What a special night, Kati! Your toast was very touching. I've never seen Hillary so relaxed. I bathe in your happiness and success."

I basked under the warm glow of Richard's gaze. Sometimes, when I rose to speak, he would touch his heart with his hand.

■ ■ ■ ■

One memorable night, Teddy Kennedy spontaneously burst into "Danny Boy," his brother Jack's favorite Irish ballad, while Adolph Green played the piano. As we were saying good night to the senator and his wife, Victoria Reggie Kennedy, Richard said, "Well, you and I sure married up, Teddy." To which Kennedy replied, "Yeah, but wasn't it fun getting there?"

Later, Senator Kennedy wrote us: "Dear Kati and Richard, Vicki and I haven't come down from the clouds after Sunday night. We are still floating along remembering an extraordinary roundup of old friends and new 'Glitteries.' . . . But most of all it was great fun because you two made it so! Your attention to detail — the seating arrangements, the entertainment, all blended into the perfect 'soiree.' The toast best of all. Your friend, Ted."

By far our most memorable times were when we hosted the man we considered the greatest figure of our time, Nelson Mandela, who stayed with us at the residence a couple of times. He was always accompanied by a tall, strapping Afrikaans aide named Zelda, who watched her boss like a hawk. Zelda would whisper, "Sir, your masseur has arrived," and Mandela would obediently rise from the table. Another time, she extracted him from a lively conversation to say, "Bob De Niro and Whoopi Goldberg are waiting to have their pictures taken with you, sir."

One of my life's greatest thrills was lending the tall but somewhat frail Mandela my arm to lean on, on the walk from the Waldorf to the United Nations. As we walked, he expressed mystification at our country's obsession with President Clinton's relationship to a White House intern. "You know, Kati," the South African president said, shaking his head, "in our country we like our men to be virile" (he pronounced the word *vir-isle*). One of my most treasured possessions is the memoir he dedicated to us, "To Ambassador Richard Holbrooke and Kati Marton — a wonderful couple who have earned our respect and admiration."

I cannot add to the volumes written about Mandela's near-miraculous humanity and genuine love of life. How different from those other leaders — from Khomeini to Milosevic to Mugabe — I have known, who missed their moment, and left only a legacy of carnage and destruction.

After attending a string of our parties, Sir

Jeremy Greenstock, the British ambassador to the UN, wrote me, "I am not sure whether you really enjoy being a diplomatic hostess, but you certainly give a great impression of doing so — so please don't stop. We seem to have been to a succession of great parties given by the Holbrookes and we are very grateful to have been included."

I was often exhausted, since by day I researched a book on presidential marriages, traveling the country to interview former First Couples and their aides. One former First Lady continued to resist my many interview requests. On March 5, 1999, the *Washington Post*'s legendary editor, Ben Bradlee, wrote me, "Damned if I didn't get a call the other day asking for a character assessment of you! The questioner stated you were writing a book about first ladies. The questioner was acting on behalf of Nancy Reagan. The questioner — what the hell — was [former director of central intelligence] Dick Helms. So I told him that your bomb-throwing days were pretty much behind you."

Thanks in no small measure to Bradlee, I did get the interview with the cautious and controlling Mrs. Reagan. She revealed a powerful personality, which strengthened my own judgment that she was one of the most influential of all our First Ladies.

On Monday, January 24, 2000, after a dinner for several African leaders, I was too exhausted to get out of bed. Richard taped this note to my mirror: "Katika! I wish I could stay in bed with you (who coughed *not once*) all morning, but [Zimbabwe president Robert] Mugabe and [Congo president Laurent] Kabila call. I will keep the evening free and we can go out for dinner. I love you so! Signed, T. PS Keep the cellphone with you so I can reach you!"

And after such a day he wanted to take me out to dinner!

We were of course bitterly disappointed by the Supreme Court's decision to stop the Florida ballot recount and hand the 2000 presidency to George W. Bush. But Richard never wasted much time on regret and might-have-beens. Back in private life, he threw himself into running the Asia Society, the American Academy in Berlin (which he had founded at the end of his tenure as ambassador to Germany), and the Global Business Coalition Against HIV/ AIDS.

I had my own share of humanitarian work with Human Rights Watch, the Committee to Protect Journalists, which I chaired for five years, and, from 2003 to 2008, as head of International Women's Health Coalition. I also began a new book about a generation of gifted Hungarians who changed the world.

Richard dreamed of new places for us to explore: Antarctica! The outer islands of Indonesia! Patagonia! But he would also say to our friends, Kati is more Kati in Paris than anywhere else. So Paris remained our place.

The Dayton Accords and his high-profile role at the UN had catapulted Richard to the world stage. It did not seem to make much difference that he no longer had a government job. In Europe, he was the American with the single name, Holbrooke. He had negotiated the end to Europe's bloodiest war since World War II. Strangers who recognized him in restaurants would send over bottles of wine or champagne. He wore it lightly. "I'm glad to be known for something real," he'd say, "not famous for being famous." He still had large ambitions, but as a historian of himself, he knew he had his place in the history books.

In Paris, we had our rituals. We usually stayed with our friends journalist Christine Ockrent and her partner, the founder of Doctors Without Borders, Bernard Kouchner. The Kouchners loaned us the top floor of their Parisian duplex, overlooking the Luxembourg Gardens. They are a remarkable couple and we formed a close foursome. Bernard, the irrepressible and irresistible raconteur and passionate humanitarian; Christine, his brilliant and lower-key partner, his perfect foil. We often dined with them at the Closerie des Lilas, so often that Richard's signature and note, "Dîner avec Christine et Bernard, au Closerie, quel rêve de Paris!" was printed on the place mats of Hemingway's fabled brasserie.

One evening, Bernard whisked us off to a little village green where old men played *boules* in the twilight: la place Dauphine — a provincial square tucked in the middle of Paris, surrounded by cafés. Montand and Signoret lived there, Bernard told us, pointing to an apartment over a café. The iconic actor, singer, and activist Yves Montand and his actress wife, Simone Signoret, were Kouchner's great friends and comrades in many human rights battles. The square is one of those Parisian secrets that catches you by surprise and to which we returned often.

Back at the Kouchners' that evening, Bernard put on a Montand CD. He and I sang along with his old friend in the background, vying to see who recalled more lyrics. Bernard knew them all. I can hear his rich baritone crooning, "Les feuilles mortes se ramassent à la pelle, Tu vois je n'ai pas oublié . . ." With Richard his rapt audience, it was a moment of perfect Parisian happiness.

Perhaps inevitably, the high drama and intense interaction of our Bosnian and UN days evolved into a more conventional union. Our tight bonds loosened. We were no longer full partners in our personal and professional lives. In 2004, Richard pitched himself headlong into the presidential campaign of his friend Senator John Kerry, writing foreign policy papers and crisscrossing the country speaking on behalf of Kerry and other Democratic candidates for office. He was itching to return to public life. At the same time, I was writing *The Great Escape: Nine Jews Who Fled Hitler and Changed the World*. Researching the lives of nine influential Budapest Jews pulled me deeper into my own and my native country's history. I was spending weeks at a time in Budapest, doing interviews and translating archival material. I loved speaking Hungarian and I was soon making new friends in Budapest — friends who had no connection to my New York life. Richard was the center of my life and we talked on the phone at least every day, wherever we were. But as our tenth anniversary approached, we began to treat each other as best friends.

Ours was a conventional story. We were on automatic pilot, and the door to temptation was ajar. I allowed someone to walk in. He was handsome, witty, and, above all, *Hungarian* at a time when I was engrossed in the history that had been kept from me for much of my life. We spoke the language of my childhood, and laughed at the same things. He knew the words to my favorite childhood song about a lonely fisherman on Lake Balaton, and he knew the word for the small crevice in the collarbone, *so tarto*, salt cellar, which my grandmother taught me. All his stories were new to me — and yet familiar. Walking into his villa in Buda, the western section of Budapest near where I had spent my childhood's most dramatic years, I recognized the faded Persian carpets, the dark oil paintings on the walls, and my parents' silver pattern. It felt like home.

A snapshot: My friend and I are driving to his country house. I spy a narrow slice of water in the far distance. I ask him to drive down to the shore of Lake Balaton. In the back of his Jeep, I pull on my bathing suit, then jump out and sprint toward the lake of my childhood. I feel something close to ecstasy as I swim farther and farther away from the shore. I am a child again paddling around this lake in an inner tube during the summer before my parents' arrest. My mother, father, and sister and I are still a family, we are still whole. I feel that if I swim far enough out, I will find that child and that family. With my friend standing and watching me from the shore, I might fulfill the primal urge to mend the broken childhood.

But like the mist that shrouds the Balaton in the early morning, that vision soon evaporated. I had made a different life. I loved a turbulent American. It was too late to undo all that.

Richard was my best friend and I could not keep anything from him for long. He had given me such confidence, such unlimited support, how could I keep our first crisis from him?

Sitting on the grass at our house in Bridgehampton, I admitted I had let a friendship go too far. We both wept. I felt small and knew I had made the biggest mistake of my life. "I told you when we got together," Richard said, "that I would have to forgive you, if something like this happened, because you are *it* for me. So, since you got us into this, you have to get us out of it." He got up and left, and I heard him drive away. But he had said, get *us* out of this. He said it was *our* problem. So I knew *we* were not over.

It would be too easy to blame this episode on my genetic inheritance. But in 2004, I did often recall the summer before my parents' arrest. My mother and father had each fallen briefly and recklessly in love: my mother with a much younger man, my father with the beautiful wife of a British diplomat. Yet from prison Papa had smuggled out a letter written with the stub of a pencil on cigarette paper: "I miss you horribly and am worried sick about you. Under no circumstances should you ever set foot in this place! Do everything in your own and the children's interest . . . and only then think about me . . . I love you more than ever, but that should not sway your decision and please forgive my stubborn stupidity in assuming we would be spared. Only you three matter. I don't. The children should forget me."

My father's letter did not reach my mother, since his cellmate was actually a state informer who took it only as far as Papa's interrogator. My father was punished with solitary confinement for trying to contact my mother — who, unbeknownst to him, was already an inmate in the same prison. My mother always said that prison saved their marriage. Having burrowed deep inside the Hungarian secret police archives in writing their story, I now understand what she meant. My parents had observed each other's behavior in prison and fell in love all over again.

Richard and I did not go to prison. But we did live our own private agonies after I confessed to a much too intense relationship with another man. When I ended that friendship, Richard wrote me, "I know it took real courage for you today. If you had not done so, our lives would have become increasingly distant and ultimately embittered beyond repair. You caused this crisis, but you have also given us another chance, even as we approach our tenth wedding anniversary. I have never had any doubt about my priority; you are still the center of my life . . . And I do love you."

He never mentioned the man, never even asked his name. He knew it was over — just as he had sensed that it was happening. He knew me better than any other human being had ever known me. And he loved me anyway! Though I continued to return to Budapest, Richard never asked if I had seen *him*. I admired and loved my husband more than ever.

Afterward, we were not quite the same couple. We had been tested. We had survived. We were each grateful to the other for making the right call. I do not recommend this kind of testing for others. But for us it was a perhaps necessary jolt. For a heartbeat, I had toyed with the idea of a more quiet life, with a less demanding, more placid soul. We faced the prospect of life without the other, and it was frightening. We never again took our eyes off the thing we prized most.

Though we may have lost some of our innocence, during the next seven years we were closer than in our first decade together. We had learned the hard way that we were irreplaceable to each other. Imperfect but irreplaceable. Who knows how to explain these things? We simply worked. I felt a supreme lightness when, on my next birthday, Richard said, "We're still stronger than dirt," as he often had before we actually knew that to be true. I knew we would be all right.

In Paris, away from Washington, away from New York and Budapest, we found each other again. A broken chair precipitated the purchase of our own Parisian place. Sometime in 2004, Richard landed with a crash on the Kouchners' parquet floor, surrounded by the wreckage of a Louis XVI fauteuil. I finally found a rationale for my old dream of Parisian real estate. "That's it," I told my husband. "We have to get our own place. We're dangerous houseguests." The Kouchners did not disagree. Richard did not see why we needed an apartment in Paris. Because I am more Kati in Paris than anywhere else, I reminded him. As usual, he was ready to indulge me.

What fun to jump on the back of Bernard's motorbike and careen around the Latin Quarter at dangerous speeds in search of a pied-à-terre. Several weeks later, my nephew Mathieu called us in New York and said he had found it. A little gem on the rue des Écoles, for a very good price. "Viens vite, Kati." "Come quickly," he said. "This will sell fast." I asked Bernard and Christine to inspect it, before I hopped a plane. "C'est parfait," Bernard pronounced. Too many people in *velours côtelé* (corduroys) in this neighborhood, said Christine — meaning academics. Down the street from the Sorbonne, the Collège de France, and the École Polytechnique, a short walk to the Jussieu Campus of the University of Paris, as well as its School of Medicine: this street isn't called rue des Écoles — the street of schools — for nothing. I was back in my old neighborhood.

I was on a plane the next day and the owner of a pied-à-terre in the Latin Quarter by the week's end. Thanks to the Kouchners, a master craftsman from Avignon named Eric soon transformed the bland walls of my small pad into the interior of a tiny *maison provençale*. Eric burnished terra-cotta and butter-yellow paint to a high sheen using a technique called *marbre de Venise*. With rosy bricks on the floor and walls, I soon had a (minuscule) French country kitchen. I was so thrilled with everything that by now the Avignon autocrat was barely even checking with me.

Each morning, while Eric and his colorful crew of Ukrainian and Moroccan workers were plastering and painting my apartment, I sprinted from the Kouchners' — where I was still staying — across the Luxembourg Gardens, up to the Pantheon, down the rue de la Montagne Ste.-Geneviève to the rue des Écoles — wild with joy that I finally owned a little piece of Paris.

Hiding lamps, little tables, and copper pots behind me, I hailed elusive cabs who grumbled at having to transport non-human cargo, as I crisscrossed the city with my treasures.

Parisian department stores do not deliver, so one Saturday my nephew Nicolas borrowed a friend's car and we filled it with dishes, tableware, sheets, towels, and a small washing machine from the Bazar de l'Hôtel de Ville, the famed BHV, on the rue de Rivoli. Nico could barely see out the windshield of the overstuffed car. I had ordered the basic furniture using Christine's catalogues, but everything nonbasic — carpets, mirrors, a round table for eating (dining was not in the cards for the simple life I planned) — I bought from neighborhood *brocantes*, a fancy name for junk shops. I felt like a student again — starting out in the same neighborhood where I had been so happy.

Luisa, the concierge of the rue des Écoles apartment, welcomed me to her castle as she would the advance party of a horde of barbarians. In cataracts of Spanish-accented French, she listed all the rules of *la maison* I was already breaking. "Faut pas faire ça, madame. Ça ne se fait pas, Madame." Can't do that that isn't done. Give her fifty euros, Bernard advised. Warm her up a bit. "C'est pour quoi, ça?" What's this for? was Luisa's reaction to my preemptive bribe, reducing me to the status of a crooked politician encountering an honest cop. "Mais, pour vous, Luisa," I stammered. "Pour vous remercier." To thank you. "Je n'ai rien fait, madame." I haven't done anything, she shrieked back. I could hardly tell her that she'd scared the living daylights out of me. So I sheepishly took back the fifty euros and waited until she had done something to earn them — which was very soon. In no time, I got used to the alarming pitch of her voice. This was her sole defense against a high-speed, high-tech world encroaching into the vanishing world of the concierge.

We have since become friends. Luisa even read my last book, when it was published in French. "Vous m'avez fait pleurer, Madame Kati." You made me cry. When I am away she turns my place into a virtual greenhouse. So fertile is her green thumb that when I return after some months' absence, I can barely see the rue des Écoles from a window lush with Luisa's botanical garden. She also rearranges my furniture, and sometimes for the better.

I did not let Richard see my handiwork until it was ready. By New Year's of 2005, we were in the apartment. He was less excited by my fabulous color scheme and amazing junk shop finds than by the neighborhood. "We have to try every single restaurant in the *cinquième!*" he said. Our choices were unlimited: Tibetan, Arab, Vietnamese, Italian, Japanese, and even a French bistro or two. Our favorite was the most romantic, and French: Le Coupe-Chou, housed in a cozy, gabled medieval house just off the rue des Écoles. For the next five years, it was ours. However late he arrived from Kabul, or any other place, however exhausted, "Let's go to Le Coupe-Chou" were often the first words he spoke.

I could hardly wait to part the curtains each morning. Looking out at the small green triangle of the Jardin de l'École Polytechnique from my bed, I felt happy at the molecular level. I could hear the sound of Luisa sweeping the courtyard, and the gallomphing of kids en route to school in the stairwell. Beneath my second-story window, the whoosh of the bus that bore the magical sign SAINT-GERMAIN-DES-PRÉS and the hum of the little green street cleaning machines that gave each day the chance for a fresh start were the background sounds to these perfect mornings. All seemed right in the world.

And so we began our exploration of our neighborhood. My hyperkinetic husband became a Parisian flaneur. There is no native English word for that quintessentially Parisian pastime, quite simply because Americans do not consider aimless ambling a legitimate occupation. In Paris *flâner* is what you do — and it is never really aimless. Any stroll in Paris brings you face-to-face with history, with beauty, and — sometimes — with violence. All of which resonated deeply with both of us.

If you make a right turn when you leave our building, you face the spires of Notre-Dame — Richard's favorite Parisian landmark, and our first morning destination. Richard was not a big-picture guy. While I would marvel, Look at the light! which he said would be my epitaph, he would focus on the kings and angels, the gargoyles and the goats' heads staring down at us from their medieval perches. He knew them all intimately, as he had books on Notre-Dame that he liked to study even in New York. The cathedral's turbulent history embodied France's own violent past, so it was always more than merely an architectural marvel to Richard. "Are you listening, Kati?" he would ask as he launched into the history of the flying buttress. I admit, I didn't always listen, but I loved his passion.

One of the few times I felt momentarily

let down by Richard was in the spring of 2004. I had just interviewed the legendary photographer Henri Cartier-Bresson in his spectacular apartment on the rue de Rivoli, overlooking the Tuileries Garden. Our conversation was supposed to be about his memories of Robert Capa, the great war photographer and cofounder, with Cartier-Bresson, of Magnum Photo. Capa was one of the nine Hungarians I was profiling in *The Great Escape*. Rather than Capa (whom he rather dismissively called a *voyou*, a scoundrel), Cartier-Bresson shifted the conversation to André Kertész, whom he called the "poetic source" of his photography. I was slightly surprised when, even though it was only eleven in the morning, he poured us each a glass of red wine. But the greater shock was still to come. Walking me to the elevator, the ninety-four-year-old legend suddenly pushed aside his walker and literally jumped me.

"You will never believe what just happened," I spluttered into the cell phone to Richard, when I got in the elevator. "As we were saying good-bye, Cartier-Bresson sprang on me with a big wet kiss. And I don't mean two pecks on the cheek." Instead of offering sympathy, Richard laughed and said, "Wow!" Admiration was pouring

211

through my cell phone. "I just hope I'm like that when I'm his age," he teased. So with a curt "Well, thanks a lot," I hung up.

Paris was the only place where Richard enjoyed shopping, and half my closet and half his are the result of those expeditions. After a lunch at the Café de Flore, we discovered 'Artwood, as we called Hartwood, on the rue du Bac. "Monsieur has exceptional shoulders!" the whippet-thin salesman in his stovepipe pants and pointy-toed shoes would marvel, running his hands across those exceptional shoulders. "We will create just the jacket for such shoulders." With a few lightning-fast strokes of his tailor's chalk, he soon transformed a cashmere blazer into an object we had no choice but to buy. At the same time, the clerk, with the appraising eyes of a Medici courtier, smoothly steered me toward a pinstriped suit, whose twin, he confided, Demi Moore had recently purchased. "Sexy but elegant," he said. "Comme madame." I have three different versions of that suit in my closet.

Holding hands, we savored marching up the red-carpeted stairs of the grandiose Quai d'Orsay — the French Ministry of Foreign Affairs — to be greeted by our

friend Bernard, the foreign minister. "Le
Roi Bernard," Richard teased him.

CHAPTER FIFTEEN

On April 5, 2005, Peter called me. "Come meet me in Central Park," he said. It was such an unusual request, I grabbed my coat and rushed out the door. Peter looked handsome and debonair as ever in his soft tweed jacket and crisp blue and white checked shirt. But his voice, strained and hoarse, had lost its rich, mellifluous timbre. His gaze was as fierce and determined as ever. Dispensing with his usual teasing banter, he took my arm and led me to the nearest bench. My heart was pounding. We had lately begun to find common ground.

"I have been diagnosed with lung cancer," he said. How could this be? This strong, handsome, still youthful man, my children's father, the lover and tormentor of my life — fatally ill. I started crying, but he raised his hand to stop me. "I'm going to fight it — and beat it." He stood up. "Let's walk," he said, and led me deeper into the park.

People approached him with broad smiles and easy familiarity. "Hey, Peter! How's it going?" He flashed his familiar smile. Passersby shot the weeping woman by his side puzzled looks. "God," I said, "they can't give you a minute of privacy. Even now." He shrugged. This was his life. He was used to it.

It was a pain-soaked spring and summer. Lizzie returned from a job she loved in Cape Town, South Africa. Peter was too sick to attend Chris's graduation with highest honors and induction into Phi Beta Kappa at Wesleyan University in Middletown, Connecticut. We drove straight from the graduation to Peter's bedside. I raised a glass of champagne. "Here's to you feeling better," I said. "Here is to me *being* better," he corrected me.

He fought like the devil, but he did not have a single good day. I will always be grateful to his wife, Kayce, for letting me visit him often. In the face of death, our old passions and battles seemed ridiculously trivial. We were a family again and we loved each other and our children.

What a gift it was for me to be with him near the end. Thus I was able to mourn his death with our children. And I still do. We had flown too close to the sun, but in Chris and Lizzie we have the best of us. The children and I speak easily and often of their father: his remarkable career, his great talent, and his self-sabotaging insecurities. He was, above all, a loving, attentive father. Our children know their parents loved each other deeply — if imperfectly — and that they were born of that love.

When Peter died in August 2005, we did not tell my father. One evening, I walked in and found Papa watching the news, tears streaming down his face. He had just seen a report about the death of his son-in-law. Papa died three months later, a year after my mother's passing.

■ ■ ■ ■

PART V

■ ■ ■ ■

Then there was the bad weather. It would come in one day when the fall was over. — Ernest Hemingway, *A Moveable Feast*

CHAPTER SIXTEEN

I have come to Paris in search of healing and distance. Paris holds memories of a time before Peter, before Richard — a time before I had children. Grief imposes its own rhythms: my feelings of loss and sadness collide with an appetite for life I've not felt since I was a girl here in 1968. I will try to live in Paris at my own pace, the way I dreamed then. Unlike in those days, I am not trying to be French. I am merely looking to live life more *mindfully*, more respectfully.

There is less tension and less excitement in my life now. Though history no longer blasts in like a gale when the front door opens and a voice calls out, "Katika!" I hope to go toward something, not just fleeing a way of life that has ended.

My corner of the Latin Quarter is not a place where I ever run into anyone from home. There is both freedom and loneliness in that dislocation. This is still the Old Paris. There are none of the glossy shops that give the boulevard St.-Germain a Madison Avenue feel. There are, however, six camping and outdoor sporting shops — geared to campers of a *certain age*, all within a mile of my apartment. A chain called Au Vieux Campeur (I love the image of the Old Camper) dominates this corner of Paris and shares it with six bookstores in two city blocks, each specializing in a different category: the Humanities, Asia, Africa, Philosophy. And then the movie theaters: nearly one on every block. Body and spirit are nourished here.

From my window, I observe the morning parade passing on the rue des Écoles. Students stream by, weighed down by heavy backpacks en route to the Sorbonne. While iPads and laptops are no doubt stuffed among their books, there is a timeless feel to these aspiring scholars. Can their dreams be so different from mine, when I wrote my parents, "I am so excited to take my place in one of those huge amphitheaters and soak in the wisdom of a great mind"?

Also passing each morning, on his way to work, is the local pharmacist. There is something reassuring about his purposeful stride, his well-worn briefcase with a leather flap tucked under his arm. He is much less imposing in baggy corduroys than the crisp white coat he wears at work. The pharmacist and I are on "Bonjour, madame, Bonjour, monsieur" terms, though for years he set aside Richard's cholesterol-lowering pills — cheaper here than in New York. *Mes condoléances*, he said the first time I entered his pharmacy after Richard's death. "My condolences," not a word more, before resuming his professional reserve. Yet when I come in with a sore throat, he takes time to probe where exactly the pain is, and whether my cough is dry or "productive," then he collects four different medicaments from his shelves and tells me which to take at what time of day for which symptom. The total comes to under fifteen dollars. As a sign of his professional pride, on his counter he keeps a framed photograph of Marie Curie, whose laboratory was nearby.

In Paris, you often trade easy American warmth for professionalism. Sometimes I miss that human connection. But I like the way Parisians imbue their work with dignity. The waiter at Café Le Rostand, where I am writing this, spins his metal tray in the air, making a half-dozen tiny cups tremble, as if he were a circus performer. Pirouetting between tables, he simultaneously slides my credit card into his little machine and leans in to the next table. "Je vous écoute, monsieur," he says, listening intently to the order that he will remember quite precisely, without writing it down. He is the master of his universe.

Each morning, I line up for bread at the Eric Kayser *boulangerie* on the rue Monge and exchange a round of "Bonjours" with the bakers and my neighbors. As I leave with my baguette, the clochard, the homeless man, who has chosen this prime spot in the warm and aromatic entrance of the bakery, recognizes me from my last visit to Paris. "Vous êtes de retour, madame!" You are back, he says. I am cheered by this, the morning's first personal greeting. I notice that his suitcase on wheels has a sticker that says *Voyager Bien.* Travel well. He has the satisfied air of a man who is doing that.

My still warm bread under my arm, I pass the cinema Desperado, on the other side of the street from my apartment. How does this theater, specializing in American films shown in the small hours on TV at home, compete with the five others within a three-block radius? Until now, I've rushed past them all, en route to more pressing business.

An orderly line waits outside the box office. There are no advance sales for the cinema Desperado. This week the theater is honoring Elizabeth Taylor, who recently passed away. But last week was a festival of screwball American comedies I had never heard of and the line was just as long. I buy my ticket for *Raintree County*. A second clerk tears my ticket in half and a third shows me to my seat in a theater that is hushed even before the credits roll. This crowd is here for a serious movie experience. It is a world away from my noisy Broadway Cineplex, where we jostle each other with giant tubs of popcorn and industrial-size cups of soda. There is no food whatsoever at the Desperado. (The French regard food as much too important to waste on snacks.) *Raintree County* is a pretty mediocre film but you wouldn't know that from the audience reaction to it. A hushed atmosphere reigns until we troop out of the theater. Then I overhear snatches of intense conversation that remind me of my old Sorbonne classes and make me think we have seen a different film.

I'd like to rush home now and tell Richard about my first neighborhood movie experience. He loved the movies! In the fall of 1993, when we were still just social friends, he was home from Germany and called to suggest a morning coffee. We mixed up the Madison Avenue café where we were to meet, and, after twenty minutes or so, we each gave up waiting. Walking up Madison Avenue in the pouring rain, annoyed I had wasted my morning, I ran into Richard. "Let's go see a movie," he suggested. "It's not even noon!" I sputtered. I would not have been more shocked had he proposed we take a room at the Carlyle Hotel across the street. I did not yet know him well and did not know that movies were his preferred means of escape — a place he wanted to take me.

I don't want to go back to my empty apartment yet. When you have the blues, motion is better than sitting still. So I head up the rue des Écoles, distracting myself with a change in route. Instead of crossing the Luxembourg Gardens, and from there to St.-Germain-des-Prés, I take the opposite direction to the rue Geoffroy St.-Hilaire. I arrive at the Paris mosque. Inside, I find a walled patio, planted with rosebushes and tiled in blue and green mosaic. People sit around tiny tables sipping tea. Though this is a secular space, it is infused with a serenity not found in a café. I order mint tea, which arrives in a small glass cup and is very sweet. Sparrows circle overhead, sometimes dipping down to pick at crumbs of baklava left on plates.

Inside, there is a Turkish bath, laid out in the traditional way. It reminds me a little of Budapest's Turkish baths, where I first learned to swim. The clients are mostly French; the masseuses are Algerian. The low hum of their Arabic conversation as they slather and knead us, the gray light that filters through the ceiling latticework, are soothing. I drift off to the sound of the tinkling fountain in this tiny Arab village inside Paris. The Algerian masseuse emits a "Mon Dieu!" at the tightness of my shoulders. "My husband died," I explain. Over the deep chasm of culture, history, language, age, and circumstance, we connect, briefly, as two women. "Eh, oui," she sighs and doubles her effort. The eternal fate of women, her strong hands seem to say. Perhaps she is a widow herself? But I am drifting off. The mosque and its *hamam* are part of my Paris life now.

At 4 P.M. on a glorious Sunday in June, I note with relief that another day is almost over. This is wrong! One day less; one more I will not get back. It is a day Richard did not have. So I will stop this business of filling up the day and start *living*. But grieving

225

is not a straight line.

I take the Métro from the Gare d'Austerlitz to meet my nephew at the Parc des Buttes-Chaumont, in the tenth arrondissement, at the far end of the city — another new destination for me. Across the aisle from me, a man is reading the Koran. Next to him an elderly Chinese lady is carrying a bag of firecrackers. In the seat in front of me, a woman dressed head to toe in bubble-gum pink commands her identically attired daughter, "Ulj le!" Sit down, in Hungarian. We are not in the Latin Quarter anymore. In fact, it doesn't even feel like the Paris I know. People watching is not something I indulged in in my former life. Richard absorbed my total attention. Nor was public transport his preferred way to get around; not when there was a waiting car outside.

When I was part of a couple, I was part of a self-contained universe. Even when I was by myself, I looked at my watch to calculate Richard's time zone. Now I observe myself and my reactions as I would a stranger. I no longer live in a protected world of waiting cars and drivers, fixers, first-class travel, and smiling customs officials speeding me past lines of travelers. Why not be bold? What more can happen to me this year? For the first time in my life there is no one I need to *please*. Just myself. My old routines have vanished with Richard.

I sign up for my life's first bus tour, the kind where a banner-waving guide with a microphone bullies a group of forlorn tourists. I joined because I wanted to see Leonardo da Vinci's *Last Supper*, in its home, in the starkly simple chapel of Santa Maria delle Grazie, in Milan. A group tour was the only way to do so. The trip takes a day and is well worth it. You cannot appreciate Da Vinci's powerful scene without standing in front of his masterpiece, where he intended it to be seen. It is much grander in scale than I expected and makes me feel as if I am having dinner with Christ and his apostles. I am struck by the fact that none of them interacts with the man who has just announced that one of them will betray him. None of the apostles puts an arm around Jesus. They seem busy protesting their own innocence. Jesus looks very alone.

I am the last one to clamber aboard the big yellow tourist bus and the guide reprimands me for holding up the group for five minutes.

I smile at the memory of my last trip to Italy, in October 2010, with Richard. Motorcycle police rose in their seats and performed balletic moves, directing traffic in front of our car as wailing sirens speeded our way to a ministerial dinner. I don't miss that part of my old life.

In a store window on the rue du Cherche-Midi, a pair of dangerously high-heeled suede pumps in a shade of red catches my eye. Would Richard approve? I automatically ask myself. Before I answer my own question, I am pointing them out to the saleslady. "Ah, oui," she says. "Évidemment," as in, how obvious. *Framboise* — raspberry is *le couleur cette saison*. A propos of *cette saison*, she exclaims, "Not since 1985 have we had such a warm fall!" She makes it sound like *1885*. Yet 1985 seems recent to me. It was the year Chris was two, and Lizzie five, and we moved into the apartment on Central Park West that I am now selling. Thinking about how quickly the last years flew by, I buy the *framboise* pumps. With such small gestures, I experiment with my new persona.

I have also started jogging. Running gives you a different connection to a city. For one thing, I normally take pains to look a certain way before I head out in Paris. Even in a neighborhood of corduroy-wearers like mine, you cannot step out of your front door without makeup, well-coiffed hair, jewelry, nice shoes, and the required scarf tied just so. There is a performance aspect to every foray onto the Parisian stage. People check each other out, frankly and without embarrassment. Even elderly retired couples in the Luxembourg look as if they are on a date. This is part of the city's pleasure. No carelessness, no sloppiness — focus on the task at hand. This soigné air gives the city its festive quality, an acknowledgment that we are in Paris.

But when you run you can be out the door in five minutes in just your sweats and running shoes and it is acceptable. People understand you are a runner. They don't inspect you, which frees you to appraise things from behind sunglasses. Somehow, the experience of running makes the city more accessible, more mine.

Early in the morning, as I jog down to the Seine via the rue des Bernardins, I am surprised to see other runners. What a thrill to have accidentally joined the world of the Left Bank jogger. As I pick up my pace toward the river a woman jumps in front of me and practically stabs me with a leaflet. "Je ne suis pas du quartier . . ." This isn't my neighborhood, I protest. "All the more

229

reason to take one, and find out about this!"
she shouts after me. Parisians are among
the world's most argumentative people — a
trait that mostly amuses me. Even if your
French is fluent, as mine is, they can smell
a foreigner and have the peerless gift for
making you feel a perfect fool. Along with
looking good, it is part of their civic duty as
Parisians.

I turn right, toward the Quai de la Tournelle, and cross the Pont de Sully, heading
toward the Bastille, turning left off the Quai
des Célestins, and cross the rue de Rivoli. I
enter the stillness of the place des Vosges,
ethereal in the early morning. The soot that
covered the graceful pavilions when I first
glimpsed them is long gone; they glow pink
in the sun. The grass in the center of the
square is still wet, but there are other runners stretching their legs against the
benches, and now so do I. Then I treat
myself to a morning café au lait at Ma Bourgogne. Richard and I used to sit here and
read the *Herald Tribune* together.

Now, ten months after Richard's death, I
am ready to venture into previously forbidden territory: the Pavillon de la Reine,
where we began our life together, during
Christmas 1993. Entering the hidden front

door, across the cobblestoned courtyard, into the rustic elegance of the gabled lobby, I feel a rush of memories: our excitement on that first visit, the sense that something important was beginning. The warmth of this country inn in the heart of Paris after five days of driving through the ice storms of the Loire enfolds me anew. During those five days of regret for the family life I was leaving, Richard and I laid the foundation for a new life. Now, back in the place where we started, I am brimming with good memories.

I head back out into the golden fall sunshine, retracing my route to the rue des Écoles. Just before I reach the river, by a small park in the shadow of the Bastille column, at the Quai des Célestins, I notice a small knot of people. A man, his long legs stretched out in front of him, is slumped against the park's chain-link fence. Blood is streaming down his face and dribbles on his shirt. A much younger woman, beautifully dressed, is pacing beside him. Several others, equally well dressed, form an anxious semicircle. The siren in the background grows louder and now an ambulance pulls up. A medic attaches an oxygen mask to the man on the ground. Two others lift him gently onto the stretcher. The young woman climbs in the back, after the stricken man. The door shuts, and, siren wailing, the ambulance takes off. Is this the heartbeat that transforms lives forever?

In Paris, life and death, beauty and violence are forever colliding. I take the rue de Poissy, a picturesque, cobblestoned street with stunning windowboxes that spill over with geraniums, toward my home. At number 5, I pass the École Maternelle. Like all French schools, it flies the French flag. But this nursery school also features a gold-lettered, black marble tablet that stops me in my tracks. "To the memory of the children — students of this school," it states, "deported from 1942 to 1944 because they were born Jewish. Victims of the Nazi barbarity with the active complicity of the Vichy government. They were exterminated in the death camps. Let us never forget them. October 5, 2002."

Facing the École Maternelle is a recently renovated Benedictine monastery, which occupies most of the block. It is spacious, airy, and well scrubbed. I wonder now, did the monks inside the beautiful monastery hear the bleat of the siren that signaled the approach of the Gestapo to collect the children from the school across the street? Did they see the black-uniformed SS and their Vichy agents lead the children from the nursery school to the waiting van? Why didn't the monks hide the children in that cavernous abbey? I hesitate to knock on the school's massive front door, though I'd like to know more about the children.

I return in the late afternoon. A teacher is leading a group of students into the monastery on a school field trip. Across the street, mothers are picking up their children from the nursery school. The front door is ajar. I walk in. Inside the vestibule, there is another black marble tablet. "Eight boys from this school," it says, "were exterminated in the Nazi death camps. Albert Aronowicz, age 7, was the youngest, and Baruch Tuchbard, age 16, the eldest." Did the school call the parents of Albert and Baruch and the others to inform them that their children weren't coming home that evening? Or had the parents already made the same journey themselves?

As I continue my deeper explorations of Paris, I am suddenly aware of these black marble plaques, and their sad message. There are over three hundred of them in the city, most of them erected since 2000.

Paris's complicated relationship with Jews feels personal to me. It was in Paris that Theodor Herzl, the spiritual father of the

State of Israel, turned zealous Zionist, while covering the trial of Captain Alfred Dreyfus in 1894. Herzl's Budapest roots closely resemble my own family's. But Herzl abandoned my parents' and grandparents' assimilationist values, and wrote *Der Judenstaat*, a cri de coeur for a Jewish homeland, fifty years before the birth of the State of Israel. Herzl felt that if religious tolerance was impossible in France, the home of the Rights of Man, it was impossible anywhere.

For a long time, the French blamed the Nazis for what happened to French Jews. And yet, as early as 1940, the French Vichy government defined Jewish status, barring Jews from all state jobs, including teaching. Vichy France published 168 laws governing Jewish life.

During the 1998 World Cup finals, I learned what a tender subject race is in France. France's victory set off an explosion of celebrations in Paris, with wildly exuberant crowds pouring into the streets, kissing strangers, and honking their horns until the early morning. It was unlike anything I have ever witnessed in New York. "How wonderful," I enthused to my French brother-in-law, "to see this multicultural team." For, indeed, the French soccer team, led by the legendary ethnic Algerian center field, Zinédine Zidane, was the very portrait of a rainbow coalition. "We do not remark on such things," my brother-in-law chided me. "They are all French." This is national policy and you will not find official French statistics on race or immigration. It would run counter to the founding principle of *la République*: the doctrine of assimilation. From the time of the French Revolution, Protestants were given equal status in Catholic France, as were Jews and the children of immigrants. Of course, the black marble plaques tell a different narrative.

Proust was a *Dreyfusard* — a supporter of the falsely accused captain — and I have lately been rereading *In Search of Lost Time*. When I first read Proust, in 1968, I was fascinated by Swann's obsessive love for Odette — a woman who wasn't even his type. Proust's depiction of love as an affliction based on an illusion struck a chord with me in those days, when I was frequently in and out of love. Now I am rereading *Swann's Way* for what Proust has to say about music, art, childhood, memory, social commentary — the human condition! Thanks to Proust, I do not beat up on myself quite as much for insufficiently appreciating the moment when it was here.

(Why didn't I tell Richard how much I adored him, was changed by him, learned from him each and every day?) That inadequacy is also part of the human condition, as Proust tells us in thousands of pages.

Late one night, as I am reading in my bedroom in the rue des Écoles, a passage strikes a deep chord with me: "Several times in the course of the year I would hear my grandfather tell at table," the Narrator relates, "the behavior of M. Swann the elder upon the death of his wife, by whose bedside he had watched, day and night. My grandfather, who had not seen him for a long time, hastened to join him at the Swanns' family property on the outskirts of Combray, and managed to entice him for a moment, weeping profusely, out of the death chamber. They took a turn or two in the park, where there was a little sunshine. Suddenly, M. Swann seized my grandfather by the arm and cried, 'Ah my dear old friend, how fortunate we are to be walking here together on such a charming day! Don't you see how pretty they are, all these trees, my hawthorns, and my new pond on which you have never congratulated me! Don't you feel this little breeze? Ah, whatever you may say, it's good to be alive all the same, my dear Amédée!' " Yes, I agree with Monsieur

Swann the elder. It is good to be alive, all the same. Proust captures the fluctuating rhythms of loss that I am daily experiencing — grief crashing against a sudden zeal for life.

This rereading of Proust leads me to that most Proustian Parisian neighborhood, the elegant provinces of the Parc Monceau, east of the Arc de Triomphe. This is another world away from my own neighborhood of schools and bookstores. The lush Parc Monceau was developed by a Jewish banker, Émile Péreire, in the late nineteenth century. The opulent mansions that surround it belonged to the great Jewish banking families, such as the Rothschilds and the Cernuschis, and others less well-known. (In fact *Monceau* is Parisian slang for nouveau riche.) Herzl himself lived at number 8, and Proust lived close by, on the rue de Courcelles. Proust was a frequent visitor to the mansion I am entering, number 63 rue de Monceau. Musée Nissim de Camondo, the discreet brass plaque indicates.

I enter a hyperrefined Proustian world furnished with the carpets, tapestries, and bibelots of the reigns of Louis XV and XVI. I picture glittering soirées in the dining room where the table is permanently set — as if awaiting Proust, Herzl, and the other great figures of the day. It is hard to conjure a more quintessentially French décor than this ode to the eighteenth century, the Age of Reason. But the host and his children and grandchildren are missing. The patriarch, Moïse de Camondo, built this temple to French civilization and left precise instructions that it would all remain untouched, as they left it — the Jewish Camondos' gift to the French nation. Moïse's son Nissim, after whom he named his museum, gave his life for France. His plane went down in flames during World War I, when he was shot photographing German military installations from the air.

Nissim's sister, Béatrice, converted to Catholicism, no doubt assuming that would protect her during the Age of Hate. In her family's mansion, with its priceless French treasures and its vast collection of Impressionist paintings — all gifts to the French Republic, as spelled out in her father's will — Béatrice may have felt safe. Her father had been awarded the Légion d'Honneur. He was a founding member of the Friends of the Paris Opera. Marcel Proust, the greatest French writer of the day, was a habitué of their salon. Why leave? So Béatrice did not heed the warning signs, as French police under SS supervision began rounding up less well-placed Jews from their schools and homes. She continued to ride her beautiful horse in the Bois de Boulogne, sometimes accompanied by a German officer. Until the summer of 1942, when the same people who seized eight children from the École Maternelle in my neighborhood arrived at her splendid house. Parisian officers packed Béatrice and her children into a wagon bound for Drancy. She and her children, Fanny and Bertrand, spent the next nine months in that grotesque antechamber to the Auschwitz-bound trains. (Drancy is just a station en route to the airport now — but an ugly stop in any weather.)

On the morning of March 10, 1943, Béatrice and her children arrived at Auschwitz — from where they never returned. They were the last of the Camondos.

Strolling now from room to opulent room, I marvel at this one-sided love affair. How blindly the Camondos, of Turkish origin, adored their adoptive country! As I drift from the parqueted salon up to the bedchambers, I search for some remnant of their pre-Parisian roots. On the mansion's top floor, there is a letter from Proust after the death of Nissim in 1917. "J'ai le coeur serré," Proust wrote with moving simplicity to Moïse Camondo, the fallen soldier's father. "My heart is clenched in pain." And, next to it, a book of Hebrew prayers, printed in 1839, and brought by the family from Constantinople to their new home, Paris. In a house furnished entirely with eighteenth-century French antiques, it is the only reminder of the Camondos' long, ultimately tragic journey.

A small silver-filigreed object once stood in our Budapest dining room sideboard and caught my eye when I was a child. It was shaped like a castle's tower, and I thought it was a toy. Then it disappeared. Years later, I saw its duplicate in the Berlin Holocaust Museum: a Jewish spice burner, the only reminder of our origins. My parents, too, had tried the camouflage of conversion and assimilation. Only in America did they find the total acceptance that eluded the Camondos, and so many others, in Paris.

Outside, in the Parc Monceau, a group of first-graders and their two teachers, one of African, the other of North African origin, sit in a circle on the lush lawn. The class itself is a multiethnic palette. Will this early exposure to the "Other" be enough to keep hate at bay?

Richard understood hate and its power to

inflame — and the speed with which it can spread from heart to heart, like fire in dry bush. He would chide me if I so much as said someone looked a certain way, whether Slav, or Latin, or Jewish. "What do you mean by that?" he'd ask in an accusatory tone. "You know it always starts with people saying things like that." Together, we had observed that skilled spewer of hate, Slobodan Milosevic, light the fire under his people. No one did more to put out that fire than Richard. I find comfort in the fullness of his life — and the satisfaction he derived from doing what he loved.

Monceau is a *parc*, and so it is permissible to take liberties with its lawn. The Luxembourg is a *jardin*, where one must never, under any circumstance, have contact with the grass. I know this, as I have stepped on that soft green carpet and had a *gardien* jump out of nowhere and call out, "La pélouse est interdite!" The lawn is forbidden. His tone implies that any fool must know this. Like the lady in Annecy with her "Mais, il y a toujours Oxford!" Obviously.

The next day, strolling through the Musée d'Orsay, I discover that my favorite paintings are from the collection left to France by the Camondo family: Degas's *The Absinthe Drinker*, Monet's *Nymphéas*, his

Rouen Cathedral series, as well as *Parliament Bridge* and Degas's *Les Repasseuses*.

The story of the Camondos haunts me for days. Partly it's because the Camondo museum feels less like a museum than an elegant home — abandoned in haste. In 1957, after a warning that my parents would be rearrested, we abandoned our own Budapest home in haste. This flight is among my childhood's most enduring memories. My most cherished possession is the painting of two Hungarian peasants, which once occupied pride of place in our Budapest home. One of the few objects we salvaged, it hangs above the mantel in my New York City apartment.

In my Paris neighborhood, France's historic fear of the Other is an inescapable fact. People mind their own business — which is mostly something I appreciate, as I do not seek unnecessary social contact just now. After five years, I have not progressed beyond the ritual *bonjour* with anyone in my building but Luisa, the concierge. When I was moving in, I stopped a strapping student who was taking the stairs two by two to her *chambre de bonne* — maid's room — on the building's top floor. Could you give me a hand moving this chest, "s'il vous plaît, mademoiselle?" She seemed happy to help, and together we hauled the cupboard to where it stands today. To show my thanks, I invited her to lunch. We spoke of her philosophy studies and of the concierge, who, she reassured me, I would come to like. I have not seen the girl since.

Indifference to the fate of those not inside their circle is the underside of the French passion for privacy, for *la discrétion*. A country that has experienced multiple invasions and a catastrophic loss of life in World War I has low expectations of humanity, and an understandable fear of *les étrangers* — strangers. "C'est normal," accompanied by a Gallic shrug, is an expression I hear often. Even death in mid-life is deemed *normal*, something to accept and live with. In New York, death is not *normal*. It is a shocking intrusion into life — a failure. No one in hyperactive Manhattan wants to be reminded of mortality.

Here in Paris, every block tells a tale and cautions the visitor against undue optimism. The past — and death — is so present in Paris because every neighborhood has some sort of a monument to the two million men — two out of every nine — lost in World War I. Every step forward is followed by one backward, the ancient stones of my neighborhood seem to say. I am reminded of that as I sit in Le Café Métro, on the place Maubert. Léon Blum, elected prime minister in 1936, was the first Jew to hold that office. He was driving through place Maubert, where I am sipping my café au lait, when a group of right-wing thugs tried to overturn his car. Did anyone sitting on this terrace move to intercede? Blum was arrested by the Gestapo. He survived Auschwitz, but his brother René did not.

What would have happened to Paris had its citizens resisted the Germans more forcefully? Would it have shared Budapest's fate — with every major building and monument bombed? It's a devastating thought: Notre-Dame pulverized like Coventry Cathedral? Still, Vichy is a name uttered with shame and as rarely as possible by the French.

My reverie is interrupted by a young man with a shaved head who leans over from the next table at the Café Métro to ask, "Can you recommend a good sushi place nearby?" He has an unmistakable Hungarian accent, so I answer in Hungarian. Again, I circle back to the scene at Parc Monceau. Will this exposure to the Other — a Hungarian skinhead looking for sushi in Paris — be enough to douse the next eruption of hate?

■ ■ ■ ■

No American writer has cast a larger shadow on this neighborhood than Ernest Hemingway. Rereading him now, I am struck by how little actual interaction there is between the author and the people of the city he is most identified with. I too have but a handful of good Parisian friends — family forms the core of my life here. But what a loss in color and interest if Parisians started behaving like New Yorkers.

In *The Sun Also Rises*, the book that made Hemingway famous, and which is partly set in Paris, there is only one exchange between the narrator, Jake Barnes, and a Parisian. She is a prostitute Jake picks up at a café. "I watched a good-looking girl walk past the table and watched her go up the street and lost sight of her, and watched another, and then saw the first one coming back again. She went by once more and I caught her eye, and she came over and sat down at the table. The waiter came up. 'Well, what will you drink?' I asked." Jake is disappointed at her lack of intellectual sparkle. "I had picked her up because of a vague sentimental idea that it would be nice to eat with someone. It was a long time since I had

245

dined with a *poule*, and I had forgotten how dull it could be."

Apart from the *poule*, Hemingway's Paris is populated mostly by Americans. It is a backdrop, a stage set, and a very good place to write. "It was a pleasant café," he wrote in *A Moveable Feast*, of his favorite, on the place St.-Michel, "warm, and clean and friendly, and I hung up my old waterproof on the coat rack to dry and put my worn and weathered felt hat on the rack above the bench and ordered a *café au lait*. The waiter brought it and I took out a notebook from the pocket of the coat and a pencil and started to write. I was writing about up in Michigan and since it was a wild, cold, blowing day it was that sort of day in the story." Parisians are of no interest to him.

I had read *A Moveable Feast*. But, as with Montaigne and Proust, I missed so much the first time. The real poignancy of *A Moveable Feast* goes right to my heart now. Hemingway's memoir is saturated with sadness and regret. He wrote it from Idaho, in late middle age. "In those days," he wrote of the Paris of his youth, "you did not really need anything, not even the rabbit's foot, but it was good to feel it in your pocket." My sister's old phone number in Richard's wallet was his rabbit's foot — and then he lost it just before he died.

Would Hemingway's memories of being young here have been less tinged with sadness had he returned — and built a new life?

It would be fun to discuss this with Richard. His absence hits me with fresh force at such moments. A feeling of abandonment taps into the first one: when I opened the nursery door to find myself alone in our Budapest apartment. But my mother returned from prison less than a year later, and eventually so did my father. We resumed our family life. Slowly, that wound healed.

As always, I am happy to pass the smiling statue of Montaigne on the rue des Écoles. His brass foot shines gold from all the hands that have rubbed it. Montaigne has re-entered my life since I first encountered him in the Grand Amphithéâtre, which his statue faces. Back then, I liked his light heart. Montaigne was irresistibly human and so interested in himself he has been called the first blogger and his *Essays* the first blog. At a time when I was also very interested in myself, he gave me permission for self-absorption.

Now I find comfort in Montaigne's views on loss, and life *after* — not *after*life. He lost his dearest friend when he was in his thirties. Montaigne embarked on his *Essays* as a way to keep his friend Étienne de La Boétie alive. People, he wrote, "should not be joined and glued to us so strongly that they cannot be detached without tearing off our skin and some part of our flesh as well." By writing about his friend, Montaigne eased his own loneliness. I am also finding joy in remembered joy. Montaigne's simple answer as to why he and La Boétie loved each other: "Because it was he, because it was I."

Having lived through France's brutal wars of religion, Montaigne advocated moderation in all things. Sociability and humanism instead of certitude and violence. Neither heaven nor hell was man's destiny. Just life here, short, unpredictable, but all we have. So we might as well make the best of it, each in our own way. That this secular humanist and I now live on the same street and see each other daily pleases me.

My neighborhood continues to reveal its mysteries. One block from my apartment is the bulky and graceless Church of St.-Nicolas-du-Chardonnet, whose chimes wake me each morning at seven. GLORIA DEO, PAX TERRAE — Glory to God, Peace on Earth — is the message chiseled above the forbidding double front doors. I am fascinated by the congregation of this neighboring church. The women and girls wear un-Parisian long, shapeless skirts, the men virtually identical, nondescript suits, while the boys are in shorts and knee socks in all seasons. One evening, I gather my courage and step inside the church. Mass is being said by an African priest, in Latin. So this is a church that defies the Vatican II reforms, which brought a dose of Montaigne's humanism to a rigid, ancient faith. Montaigne, with his generous acceptance of all things human, would not be surprised that this outpost of reaction thrives one block from the cinema Desperado.

This fall week, a long line of dark blue buses holding the CRS — the dreaded Compagnies Républicaines de Sécurité — snakes around my block. They anticipate a big *manif*. When one of the doors suddenly opens, I peer in. Same muscular body types I recall from my first sighting of them in May 1968. Same extraterrestrial aspect to their full-body padding. But these modern-day gladiators are hunched over their iPhones and BlackBerrys, awaiting their orders. I am not afraid of these riot police anymore. They too are part of my neighborhood. I have observed them summoned for protesting nurses, schoolteachers, and farmers — part of the street theater of French policing. *CRS assassin!* I recall chanting with my fellow students at the Sorbonne, less from conviction than to *go along*.

It is liberating to care less about the impression I am making. Partly that is the gift of dislocation (New York is still home). The past should not imprison you, Richard used to say when speaking to Balkan leaders stuck in the mud of their violent history. He would be telling me the same thing now. At his wake, one of Richard's aides, Vali Nasr, asked plaintively, "Now who will get the best from me?" After seventeen years with Richard, I think I know how to get the best from myself. That was his most generous gift.

In Paris, I live more intensely in the present. The pearl-gray light on winter mornings, molting briefly into apricot and violet just before sunset, moves me as much as when I first arrived, an unformed girl. The scent of chestnut trees in summer, hot chestnuts in winter, coffee at all seasons, the unique aroma of the Métro — which has its own hold on memory and time — these are my small pleasures. The days seem longer here, even in winter. At six in the evening, I sit in a café and write. Cafés are the finest places for people alone not to feel lonely. In Paris you smile only when you have something to smile about. Sorrow and pain are deemed part of life.

October 1 — I awoke this morning with a dream so vivid I wrote it down. (Richard always said, "Write it down!" when I had a thought he found interesting.) In this dream, I am on a train, a stranger next to me. I have my hand on her very pregnant belly. I feel her baby moving and kicking under my hand. It is my first dream of life this year.

Sitting on the terrace of the Closerie des Lilas with Bernard Kouchner, we both feel Richard's absence sharply but do not want to abandon our habit of meeting here. "I told him," Bernard shakes his head, "that Afghanistan was hopeless. But he did not listen to me." He shrugs. For a moment I feel compelled to argue Richard's position. That he never accepted that anything was hopeless, felt there was always *something* that could be done. But I resist. I am trying to live my own life now, as he lived his.

Leaning over to inhale the Closerie's

fabled lilac bushes, I am surprised to discover they have absolutely no smell. Did Sadegh Ghotbzadeh notice this? Did Peter, or my father? Or, for that matter, did Hemingway, who wrote in *The Sun Also Rises*, " 'We might as well go to the Closerie,' Brett said . . . Sitting out on the terraces of the Lilas, Brett ordered whiskey and soda and I took one too . . . Brett looked at me. 'I was a fool to go away,' she said. 'One's an ass to leave Paris.' "

It is when I feel happiest, and forget for an instant that this is my life now, and perhaps forever, that the loss hits with a concussive force.

In the Luxembourg Gardens, I am daily impressed by the acrobatic skills of amorous couples in wrought-iron chairs. They turn them into a chaise longue by pushing them together, or tip them back so their canoodling is almost horizontal. But it is an elderly couple that transfixes me. Dignified and unhurried, they hold hands as they stroll on the gravel path beneath an alley of chestnut trees. Unsmiling, they share expressions of mutual contentment. Another couple, in another Parisian park, comes to mind: the photo Richard carried in his wallet for seventeen years of the two of us, in the Tuileries Garden, giddy with newfound love, which disappeared shortly before he did. We will never be this elderly couple in the winter sunshine.

I am writing this at the café Le Rostand. From here, I can see my old apartment and the French windows I used to fling open each morning, inhaling the sounds and smells of Paris.

In the warmth of a winter morning, I am suddenly filled with inexplicable joy. How fortunate I have been in love from my parents, Peter, and Richard.

Could anyone ask for better preparation for the next chapter of life than these: my mother doing sit-ups in her communist cell; my father, who twice lost everything, first to the Nazis, then the communists, rebuilding his life in America.

My beloved Richard was exhausting and demanding. He worked too hard, and left too early. It was at times a challenge to create space in his world — so crowded with public men and women — for the two of us. Richard was a complicated man, but he loved simply. He said we were stronger than dirt. Now I will try to be.

CHAPTER SEVENTEEN

Almost eighteen years to the day after I jumped in Richard's armored car and headed for Chartres, my daughter and I return to the great cathedral. We have located Malcolm Miller, the legendary tour guide whom Richard tried and failed to catch during our first lunch at La Vieille Maison. Sitting in the cold immensity of the cathedral, Lizzie and I wait for the famous guide. In no time, Chartres casts its spell. It is 1993 and I am sitting in the silent, beautiful church, bereft at the life I have just left behind, uncertain about the future. Richard is beside me. He has no doubt about our future and whispers urgently, "Just imagine the pilgrims' first reaction to the sight of these windows!" We spoke of a time when life really was nasty, short, and brutish, and how thousands of men — none of whose names are carved into the cathedral's soaring columns — built

254

this, their hedge against mortality. We began building our own new life that day.

The long-awaited guide, who has spent the last fifty-four years studying, marveling, and explaining this wonder, finally arrives, from his sickbed, he tells us. Chartres is Miller's private fiefdom and, with red-rimmed eyes, he surveys the knot of pilgrims lined up for his tour. "What do you want to know about Chartres?" he suddenly asks Lizzie and me. "We have forty-five minutes," he tells us. "I have waited eighteen years for this tour," I answer, and tell him about Richard walking through the restaurant's glass door to try to catch him, Christmas week, 1993. He seems neither surprised nor moved by this, listing Richard Nixon, Henry Kissinger, and Elizabeth Dole as American public figures he has guided.

When Miller launches into the story of one of his favorite stained-glass windows, depicting the Good Samaritan and Adam and Eve, I understand why Richard was determined I should have his tour. Suddenly I *get* the point of these gorgeous windows, beyond their jewellike beauty. They were a teaching tool about the Bible and a panoramic history of the Middle Ages. Listening to Miller, a world of knights, highwaymen, furriers, carpenters, and blacksmiths

— all depicted in the windows, along with scenes from the New Testament — leaps vividly to life. Popping Fisherman's Friend lozenges (as Peter used to, before he gave up smoking), Miller pokes fun at those who can't separate religion from myth and art. "They say God created the universe in seven days," he sniffs. "Really, now!" He recalls visiting a Southern Baptist once in Texas. "All he wanted to know — and he asked me several times very aggressively — was, did I have any alcohol on me! I wanted to tell him Jesus drank wine."

Our time with Malcolm Miller up, Lizzie and I light a candle for Richard and place it on a bank where scores of other tiny flames flicker in the cathedral's darkening nave. Stepping out into the silver twilight, we inhale air pungent from smoke that rises from red-tiled roofs. The little town in the shadow of the great church is withdrawing into winter slumber, just as it has for centuries. We smile in silent acknowledgment: Richard would be so pleased we made this trip and had the tour he wanted for me during our first day together. "This was for you, Richard," my daughter says, as we link arms.

What a remarkably resilient organism a family can be. In my early childhood, when we lived in a hostile environment and my parents were officially Enemies of the People, there were just four of us, and we were very close. In America, those tight family bonds loosened. Once my sister and I married and had our own families, we mutated into new units. Now, after multiple losses — mine, my children's, and my siblings — we are again close, as we were when family was all we had. We tell stories of these large personalities — our parents, my children's father, Richard. We laugh and cry and bring them along with us. No one is exempt from loss. But loss opens up space for a different life.

For the first time since Richard and I began our journey, we are all celebrating Christmas in Paris. My brother and sister, our children and my sister's new grandson are starting new traditions, and Paris offers dazzling diversions for three generations. At Ma Bourgogne restaurant on the place des Vosges we form a noisy group. My children and nephews order steak tartare, the favorite of the man they call variously *le Patron* or *l'Oncle Richard*. Imitating his elders' many wineglass-clinking toasts, Lucien, my nephew Mathieu's two-year-old son, smashes his own glass on the floor. While his parents scold him for this "*caprice*," Ma Bourgogne's smiling *patronne* quickly replaces the broken glass and coaxes her enormous golden retriever to our table for the teary Lucien to pet.

In Paris, I love my lazy mornings spent reading in bed, one eye on the street parade beneath my window. Christmas week, the creaking parquet alerts me that my son Chris is up early. So I too quickly pull on my jeans and join him, heading out into the quiet early morning darkness of the Latin Quarter. As we cross the Seine toward the Île St.-Louis, pink brushstrokes streak the black sky. Walking briskly to keep the chill away, with my son beside me, I feel an unaccustomed lightness. On the rue Jean-du-Bellay, we find a perfect café — already humming with life. Over our café au lait and buttered baguettes, we find an ease of conversation that we have not shared since he was small. This renewed closeness — partly a result of loss, partly the confined living space of my pied-à-terre — is my unexpected Christmas gift. Between Christmas and New Year's, we return to the café every morning.

I had already received another equally

unexpected gift. The evening before I left New York for Christmas in Paris, I ran into a friend of Richard's at a party. Mike Abramowitz told me he had dinner with my husband the night before he collapsed, on December 10, 2010. "He was his usual engaged self. For three hours Richard and I talked about every topic under the sun, from Afghanistan/Pakistan to Washington gossip. He spent a great deal of time talking about you," Abramowitz said. "About his pride and his love for you." Most important, Abramowitz said, "There was no sign of any illness at all when I dropped him off at your Georgetown house at ten-thirty. None."

My final conversation with Richard — his call from the ambulance — was exactly twelve hours later.

In 1995, shortly before we got married, Richard and I paid a call on one of his most revered mentors, Clark Clifford. One of the last of the great Washington Wise Men, whose biography Richard had coauthored, Clifford lived alone, on Rockville Pike, Maryland. We waited for him in the living room of his spacious colonial farm house. The once tall and imposing titan of Washington — President Truman's confidant and LBJ's defense secretary — descended the stairs with agonizing slowness. Bent over his cane, he made his way, one noisy step at a time. Peering up at us with his signature smile, his manners still impeccable, Clifford made it seem as if walking at 180 degrees to the ground was perfectly unremarkable. Afterward, Richard was quiet for a long time. Clifford sent us a beautiful silver caviar dish as a wedding gift, but by the time I wrote him a thank-you note, he had passed away.

Richard would not have easily borne such infirmity in old age.

On New Year's Eve, the whole family is gathered at my sister's apartment. My brother, Andrew, is pounding out Neil Young's "Harvest Moon," a song I love, on the piano.

there's a full moon risin',
let's go dancin' in the light . . .
Because I'm still in love with you
I want to see you dance again . . .

An almost suffocating wave of sadness washes over me. I don't want to spoil my family's exuberant mood, nor am I able to articulate why grief should strike again, in the midst of so much warmth and love. A new year beginning pulls Richard farther away from me. It begins my second year without him, without us. I head quietly for the front door, and text them from the Métro that I am sorry, but I can't do New Year's this year.

I have no desire to reflect on the significance of the year ending — as I normally would. No wish to recall its surreal start, standing on the stage of the Kennedy Center, facing a sea of mourners, President Obama's arm around me.

So I pretend it's just another evening, and spend it alone. I make dinner for myself and watch Monty Python's *The Life of Brian*, which always makes me laugh. An ordinary evening, as I begin a more ordinary life. I am barely awake when the church bells toll midnight.

The next morning, I stand in line for bread. My neighbors look much less rested than I. With his long face and flowing beard, the homeless man occupying his spot in front of the bakery is the image of an Old Testament prophet. This morning, he is wearing a blue T-shirt with a sailboat motif, and has a Christmas garland wrapped around his neck. To a captive audience of people waiting for their fresh baguettes, he expounds on President Sarkozy's New

Year's Eve message. "He tried to sound optimistic," the clochard says of the president, "but he was unconvincing. Nevertheless" — he looks straight at me — "I think we will have a good year."

ACKNOWLEDGMENTS

This book is partly based on a journal I began following my husband's sudden death. The letters to my parents and to Peter Jennings were an unexpected windfall, born of my need to sell my home of twenty-seven years. In the process of culling an Everest of accumulated possessions, I stumbled on long-forgotten letters kept by my parents and Peter, which triggered memories of my early Parisian life, first as a student, and then as a foreign correspondent.

I wrote the first rough draft of this book in the sublime sanctuary of the Rockefeller Foundation's Bellagio residence, on Lake Como, Italy. I am grateful to Steven Heintz, President of the Rockefeller Brothers Fund, and Judith Rodin, President of the Rockefeller Foundation, for their help in arranging this residency for me.

Throughout this past pain-drenched year,

my agent, Amanda Urban, has been my steady and wise friend. This is our seventh book together, and I cannot imagine my writing life without Binky's remarkable combination of loving support and determination to coax the best from me.

This is my third book with the brilliant Alice Mayhew. Alice was patient as I searched to find my voice in a new medium: a memoir. I am blessed with an editor who believes in me and imbues each new project with the excitement of the first.

Alice and the Simon & Schuster team of Jackie Seow, Nancy Singer, Gypsy da Silva, Julia Prosser, Karyn Marcus, and Jon Cox are the best in the business, and I feel privileged to work with them.

Jonathan Karp's early enthusiasm for this book gave me — and the project — a great lift.

Larissa MacFarquhar, a wonderful writer and generous friend, was my first reader and made important suggestions. Richard Bernstein, Eliza Griswold, and George Packer took time from their own books to improve mine in so many ways — and to keep my spirits up through this hard year.

My assistant, Loryn Hatch, has been a calm presence as my life was upended. I thank Loryn for her remarkable efficiency, humanity, and intelligence.

My Paris family: my sister, Julia; my nephews Mathieu and Nicolas; as well as Sabine and the irresistible Lucien, poured love, wine, laughter, and shared tears. My brother, Andrew, provided the background music to family gatherings.

My beloved friends Bernard Kouchner and Christine Ockrent defined Paris for Richard and me. As Richard once scribbled on the Closerie de Lilas place mat, "Dîner avec Christine et Bernard, au Closerie, quel rêve de Paris!" We were a rare foursome and have now become a loving trio.

Finally, I could not have gotten through the year following Richard's death, nor written this book, without my children Elizabeth Jennings and Christopher Jennings' loving support. It was essential for me that they read and approve of this work, as they, and their father, are part of the narrative. I have dedicated this work to Richard, but it is really for all my family, those present, and those who are present in these pages. It is my way of keeping them close.

I missed Richard every step of the way.

ABOUT THE AUTHOR

Kati Marton is the author of seven books, most recently, *Enemies of the People: My Family's Journey to America*, a National Book Critics Circle Award finalist and the subject of an upcoming motion picture. Her other books include *The Great Escape: Nine Jews Who Fled Hitler and Changed the World*; the *New York Times* bestseller *Hidden Power: Presidential Marriages That Shaped Our History*; *Wallenberg*; *The Polk Conspiracy*; and *A Death in Jerusalem*. She is an award-winning former NPR and ABC News correspondent. She lives in New York City.

The employees of Thorndike Press hope you have enjoyed this Large Print book. All our Thorndike, Wheeler, and Kennebec Large Print titles are designed for easy reading, and all our books are made to last. Other Thorndike Press Large Print books are available at your library, through selected bookstores, or directly from us.

For information about titles, please call:
  (800) 223-1244

or visit our Web site at:
  http://gale.cengage.com/thorndike

To share your comments, please write:
  Publisher
  Thorndike Press
  10 Water St., Suite 310
  Waterville, ME 04901